Effective

School

Boards

Effective School Boards

Strategies for Improving Board Performance

Eugene R. Smoley, Jr.

Jossey-Bass Publishers
San Francisco

An electronic adaptation of this book and the self-assessment tool is provided through the support of the National School Boards Foundation on the National School Boards Association's Resource Exchange Network at www.nsba.org.

Text excerpt on p. 97 is from Butler, Hirsch and Swift, Board Information Systems, The Cheswick Center, Rockville, Maryland, 1995, p. 69. Used by permission of L. M. Butler.

List on pp. 99–100 is adapted from Butler, Hirsch and Swift, Board Information Systems, The Cheswick Center, Rockville, Maryland, 1995. Used by permission of L. M. Butler.

Quote on pp. 102–103 is from a telephone interview with Vic Cottrell, Ph.D., Ventures for Excellence, Inc., Lincoln, Nebraska. Used by permission of Vic Cottrell, Ph.D.

Appendix B is adapted from material originally developed by the Center for Higher Education Governance and Leadership, University of Maryland, College Park, under funding by the Lilly Endowment. Used by permission of Tom Holland.

Jossey-Bass books and products are available through most bookstores. To contact Jossey-Bass directly, call (888) 378-2537, fax to (800) 605-2665, or visit our website at www.josseybass.com.

Substantial discounts on bulk quantities of Jossey-Bass books are available to corporations, professional associations, and other organizations. For details and discount information, contact the special sales department at Jossey-Bass.

Manufactured in the United States of America.

Library of Congress Cataloging-in-Publication Data

Smoley, Eugene R.
    Effective school boards : strategies for improving board performance / Eugene R. Smoley. — 1st ed.
      p. cm. — (The Jossey-Bass education series)
    Includes bibliographical references.
    ISBN 0–7879–4692–3
    1. School boards—United States. I. Title. II. Series. LB2831 .S64 1999
    379.1′531′0973—dc21
                                                     98–58158

FIRST EDITION
PB Printing   10 9 8 7 6 5 4 3 2 1

The Jossey-Bass Education Series

Contents

List of Exhibits

Preface

SCHOOL BOARDS are here to stay. They provide a practical expression of a community's involvement with its schools—a value that is deeply rooted in our society. Unfortunately, many boards do not operate as effectively as they could. Criticism of the school board, often justified, can be heard in many communities.

We must take the criticism seriously because school boards are so influential. Approximately 95,000 school board members bear the responsibility for the operation of nearly 15,000 school districts across the United States. A minority of board members, about 26 percent, oversee districts with more than 2,500 students; these districts serve some 80 percent of this country's public school students. Board responsibilities in the largest districts—those with more than 10,000 students—are especially weighty. These districts are typically (but not always) more urban, ethnically diverse communities with a higher percentage of at-risk children.[1]

Criticism of Boards

To have so much responsibility, school board members are often remarkably ill-prepared for service. About 40 percent of those currently in office have only three or fewer years of service. And they are volunteers. They run for office out of a general concern for the state of schools and the need for change in current practices. However, once in office they find the job demanding and complex. They are immersed in a set of legal and financial issues that few have the background to fully understand. They are expected to provide leadership when educational concepts are changing, complicated, and conflicting. Pressures from constituents are strong and emotional.

Experts have been increasingly critical of school boards and their ability to function effectively. They see boards as unable to focus on policy, enmeshed in the details of personnel and student discipline, and unable to lead educational reforms. Some experts suggest changing to other forms of governance that provide the opportunity for greater policy focus.[2] In some urban areas, cities and states have echoed this rejection of school boards and replaced them with control boards and advisory boards, or they have made schools a part of city government.[3]

I disagree with those experts. *I do not favor replacing school boards with other forms of governance.* My experience as a student of governance and consultant to school districts has led me to conclude that keeping—and improving—our boards is the best option. Community control of schools is central to the vitality of our democratic way of life. School boards, both elected and appointed, remain the best vehicle for this community control.

How This Book Can Help

Although this book cannot help all board members counter all criticism, it can show how board performance can be improved. For example, poor performance can come from members' confusion about their duties; it can come from a contentious and divisive decision-making process; it can come from a lack of understanding of the board's role as it relates to the role of the superintendent—just to name a few possibilities. Any one of these problems can adversely affect board performance. All of these problems—and many more—are discussed in the chapters to follow.

This book provides clear-cut guidance for board members who wish to improve. In fact, everyone who cares about how effectively boards perform, whether currently serving on a board or not, will find something useful here, ranging from an analysis of why boards fail to presentation of a model for success—the Model for School Board Effectiveness—that is based on real-life experience. Members can implement the model and maximize their own chances for success.

Rationale and Method of the Book

In my search for ways to help boards get better, I have addressed two fundamental questions: *What does an effective school board look like?* (Part One) and *How can a board, with the support of its superintendent and community, become more effective?* (Part Two). To get some answers, I have turned to experts and to school board members themselves. This book takes their experience with effective action and builds the Model for School Board Effectiveness.

The model describes the six categories of school board action, as shown in Exhibit P.1. For each of these areas, I have shown the specific characteristics that define effectiveness:

- Board decisions are rational, informed by data and full discussion.

- Boards exhibit the characteristics of well-functioning groups: a feeling of cohesiveness and of sharing goals and values.

- Board members exercise their authority discreetly and stand firm when they must.

- Boards connect with the community informally, as well as by an established formal process.

- Boards work toward self-improvement, assist new members, reflect on their responsibilities, and seek assistance when they need it.

- Board actions are strategic, matching long-term plans with immediate actions, focusing on results, and adjusting to new situations.

School Board Effectiveness Project

Much of the information and many of the analyses and recommendations in this book are an outgrowth of the School Board Effectiveness Project, which I began in 1993. The project was funded by the Good Samaritan Foundation. I began by surveying school board members, asking them about three topics:

1. What did they know about a statewide initiative to define and measure progress against curriculum standards?

2. How did they assess the operation of their own boards?

3. What were their priorities for their own improvement?[4]

The most interesting results emerged from the self-assessment portion of our survey. I found that boards did not rate themselves highly on the criteria suggested. However, they raised questions that made me skeptical of the criteria used in assessing their effectiveness.[5] This provided the context for the work reported in this book. That work draws on extensive individual interviews with forty-five school board members across the state of Delaware—nearly 40 percent of board members statewide. The interviewees described specific occasions when they felt their boards carried out their responsibilities effectively.

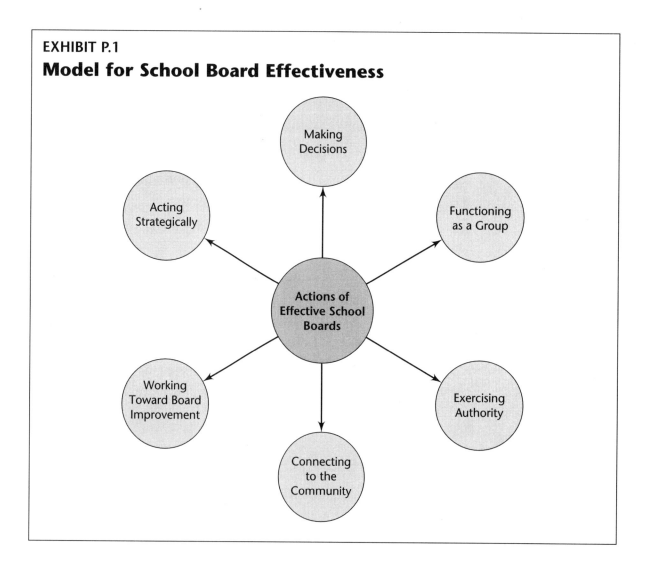

EXHIBIT P.1
Model for School Board Effectiveness

The centerpiece of my interviews was a series of questions about specific incidents that board members remembered as significant; the incidents ranged from superintendent selection to student suspensions to staff reductions. I probed who was involved, what happened, and why. I asked what the boards set out to accomplish and why the members considered their board's actions to be effective. I made every effort to elicit their opinions on just what attributes of their board enabled members to handle these situations effectively.

From these interviews I collected 111 vignettes, with commentary, that describe effectiveness in the eyes of school board members. After examining these stories in great detail, I broke the descriptions down into six areas of school board action that represent effectiveness as defined in the members' own words. Using excerpts from these vignettes to support and explain my analysis, I include many of these detailed descriptions in the chapters of this book and use my analysis of their descriptions, supplemented by my work with school boards across the country and conversations with experts, to build the Model for School Board Effectiveness that I present. This analysis offers board members, new and old, an opportunity to reflect on their own actions and judge them against the model. (See Appendix A for more discussion of methodology.)

Organization of the Book

The book is in two parts. Part One opens with the Introduction, which describes the issues facing school boards today and the major reasons school boards fail. Each chapter that follows in Part One—Chapters One through Six—describes one of the six elements of board action that are included in the Model for School Board Effectiveness.

Chapter One describes a decision-making process with a variety of distinctive characteristics: it is rational and informed by data and full discussion; members maintain flexibility and objectivity when considering the merits of alternative courses of action; the process works toward a consensus of views rather than a majority vote.

In Chapter Two, interviewees describe a shared respect and trust that recognizes the contribution of each board member. The effective board has many characteristics of well-functioning groups: cohesiveness and a sense of working together, shared goals and values, leadership within the board (often the board president), and a shared understanding and agreement on operating rules.

Chapter Three presents board members speaking of their effective activities in the context of their superintendent's recommendations and actions. There is support for the chief executive but a sensitivity about not being a rubber-stamp board. Board members cite examples of effectiveness when they initiated actions, overruled the superintendent, or withstood the pressure of staff, community, and government.

In Chapter Four, board members cite their actions in maintaining a multifaceted relationship with the community. This relationship includes informal conversation and structured input from the community, as well as board presentations to the community. Board members serve as a conduit between the school district and community.

Chapter Five shows interviewees discussing activities that help new members understand their responsibilities. They describe actions that include reflecting on and adjusting to board responsibilities and authority. They seek outside assistance and cultivate leadership and membership on the board.

In Chapter Six board members discuss and resolve the issues that are central to helping children learn. The members plan systematically and long term, taking into consideration the needs and concerns of internal and external constituents; they balance substantive and political realities; they match plans against results; they organize responsibilities and authority between superintendent and board, adjusting for strengths and weaknesses.

In Part Two I show what steps boards can take to become more effective. In Chapters Seven and Eight, I discuss how boards can best use the two sources of help they have: the superintendent and the information they get—information they depend on to guide their thinking about issues. Then Chapter Nine builds the case for board development, showing why boards should spend time and money for reflection and self-improvement. The chapter describes various approaches to board development, based on the Model for School Board Effectiveness described in Part One. Also in this chapter I describe a self-evaluation instrument based on this effectiveness model and outline processes for conducting self-evaluation, monitoring progress, and keeping track of board development—all as approaches to board improvement.

Finally, in the Conclusion I summarize the steps boards can take to improve effectiveness. First, I outline specific steps boards may consider as they work to improve their effectiveness—steps related to each of the six elements of the model. Then I describe the conclusions of my investigation and their implications for board action.

Acknowledgments

I was most fortunate to have had the financial assistance of the Good Samaritan Foundation in conducting research for the School Board Effectiveness Project. Without the foundation's support the project would not have been possible. The University of Delaware and the Delaware School Boards Association were also important contributors to my connection with Delaware and its school boards and districts. In particular, I am most grateful to the many dedicated men and women—the school board members of Delaware districts—who were candid and insightful in sharing their experiences.

The idea for this book and much of its conceptual underpinning emerged from discussions among a special group of colleagues who form the Cheswick Center. This research and education trust, based in Rockville, Maryland, includes more than a dozen senior executives, researchers, and consultants; it is devoted to helping nonprofit boards improve their effectiveness. Extending the concept of nonprofit board effectiveness to school boards was a natural outgrowth of these discussions. I owe a particular debt of gratitude to Henry Sherrill, who formed the Cheswick Center twenty-seven years ago. He saw the value of extending its concepts to school boards and provided moral support to the effort. The writings of Cheswick Senior Fellows Larry Butler, Dick Chait, Tom Holland, Thom Savage, and Barbara Taylor reflect my particular intellectual debt to their thinking and research.

I particularly want to acknowledge the role of the National School Boards Foundation as a partner in the application and distribution of this work. Their contribution significantly extends its potential use by school board members and other practitioners and educators across the country. Through their support an electronic version of this work will be available on the National School Boards Association's Resource Exchange Network at www.nsba.org.

I am grateful to Juan Fonseca for his excellent support as a research assistant during the interviewing phase of the project. I want to thank Mary Anne Hess, a perceptive and knowledgeable writer and editor, who gently and persuasively helped to improve this text. Finally, and most important, I want to note that my wife Betsy's steady, quiet encouragement and forbearance has made all the difference in the satisfaction I have felt in being able to undertake this project.

The Author

EUGENE R. SMOLEY, JR., is associate professor of educational leadership at the University of Delaware and a senior fellow of The Cheswick Center, a research and education trust based in Rockville, Maryland, that conducts research and provides consulting assistance for the improvement of nonprofit governance. He has also been a vice president of Towers Perrin, an international human resources consulting firm, where he continues to serve clients. His consulting assignments emphasize various aspects of governance, organizational analysis, operations, academic management, human resources, and strategic planning.

Smoley has assisted the presidents and boards of many educational organizations in studies of governance and management. He recently completed an assignment for the Association of Governing Boards of Colleges and Universities as director of the Commission on the Academic Presidency. The commission report addresses the opportunity for trustees, state governments, college faculty, and others to contribute to the quality and performance of the presidency as institutions of higher education address the challenges of the next decade.

Smoley has worked with school boards and superintendents on comprehensive governance and management studies of many districts, both large and small. His recent work with school boards has focused on the issue of what makes school boards effective. Working at the University of Delaware, under a grant from the Good Samaritan Foundation, he developed a model for school board effectiveness through extensive interviews with school board members. *Effective School Boards* is the result of this work. In addition, Smoley has completed a study and publication for the

National Center for Nonprofit Boards on *School Board Development: Needs and Opportunities.*

Smoley holds a B.A. in mathematics from Cornell University, as well as an M.A.T. and a Ph.D., with concentration on the sociology and politics of educational organizations, from The Johns Hopkins University.

Effective
School
Boards

Why School Boards Fail

BOARDS OF EDUCATION are a fixture of school governance, but they are not immune to criticism. In fact, their effectiveness has come under increasing scrutiny over the past decade, particularly since the 1992 publication of the influential report, *Governing Public Schools: New Times, New Requirements.*[1] That report, which suggests a reassessment of school board governance, has prompted a steady stream of articles and studies scrutinizing the role of school boards, their ability to govern, and their contribution to education reform.

Most reports about school governance acknowledge the historic and cultural importance of the school board as a bridge between a community and its schools. At the same time, critics cite low voter turnout in school board elections as compromising boards' real democratic value and fostering the tyranny of small, intensely active, single-issue constituency groups. These studies describe the significant changes occurring in school policy—the emphasis on standards and student outcomes and the increasing connection between the state and the schools in each district of the state. They cite the growing influence of subject-based organizations on curriculum reform. They acknowledge the growing diversity of our society and the struggle of boards to cope with disparate values in fashioning policy alternatives. And there is recognition of the heavy workload of school boards and the administrative nature of much of this work.

When all is said and done, school boards fail for three reasons: (1) they work in a difficult situation, with conflict and misunderstanding among board, superintendent, and community; (2) their role is unclear and misunderstood; and (3) in district after district, they repeat a handful of practical errors that interfere with their effectiveness.

The Challenge of School Board Governance

A school board is part of the community it serves. The challenge of school board governance is, in large measure, a challenge of community. Communities have become less consensual, with greater diversity in ethnic background and values. And the political structure supporting school board elections is weak. A small percentage of citizens vote in board elections, and the issues around board elections tend to be contentious and personal rather than focused on broad educational policy. So boards must govern on behalf of communities where it is difficult to build understanding of important issues and even more difficult to reach consensus on a plan of action. Citizens lack confidence in the schools and become suspicious of the very board members they elect.

School boards are also designated representatives of the state, as the state has responsibility for education and delegates authority for the operation of school districts to local school boards. State and federal governments have developed programs, standards, and outcome-based testing programs that have proscribed the operation of the local district and the authority of the local board. This further complicates the school board's relationship with its community, particularly where the community may not support the state requirements. The community sees the school board as powerless to control certain central elements of the educational program, and this undermines the community's regard for school board governance.

The job of a school board member is difficult; it is time consuming, contentious, stressful, and sometimes distasteful. Citizens are not always civil; emotions run high; issues are difficult to resolve. And because the school board member is an unpaid volunteer, it is often difficult to get the highest-quality people to run for the office. And perhaps unfairly, the community's view of the school board is often based on its perception of the quality of school board members.

Partisan community groups can make life difficult for school boards. While boards must listen to disparate opinions and try to forge consensus among competing and conflicting viewpoints within the community, they are often subjected to uncivil and personalized treatment. School board members cite the frustration of functioning in this environment:

> What is particularly frustrating is the distrust from people who elected me. I was one of the citizens until I was elected; then I became one of "them." You do something that is open to the public; then it comes back as not understood. For example, we approved $30,000 from food money surplus for a point of sale system for food service. One other board member proposed it,

and I seconded it and asked questions about it. Then it passed
unanimously. But the next day, my wife got a question at the
grocery store asking how we could spend $30,000 when we
were broke.*

Every day brings a fresh newspaper account of public controversy surrounding the schools and the difficult climate for board action created by
those who oppose board decisions. For example, the *New York Times*
reported a Santa Barbara, California, school board decision to end bilingual education. Six hundred people came to the meeting. The board's five
members said they were haunted by accusations that the proposal before
them amounted to "ethnic cleansing" and posted six police officers in the
auditorium. And when it was finally time for the vote, several dozen pro-
ponents of bilingual education moved within a few feet of the board members and glared at them.[2]

Prospective board members consider the likely abuse they will endure
if they run for office. Current board members think carefully before run-
ning for a second term.

The relationship with the community is not the only stumbling block
for boards. Member comments also reflect the importance and sometimes
the difficulty of the superintendent-board relationship.

I go to see the superintendent. He's tactful, but other board
members won't get involved. For example, I went to the superintendent about a snow day; other districts announced they
were closed; ours did not. He said the radio made a mistake.
His tone was patronizing. I'm not able to get items looked at.
The administration has their own agenda and works at their
own pace. A board member will visit a school and go back to
the administration asking why we are doing things as we are.
The superintendent says we cannot vote on an item we
observed because it constitutes prior knowledge and there's a
conflict and we can't vote.

The unrealized capacity for board-superintendent partnership in
the governance of school districts represents a major barrier to board
effectiveness.

The superintendent is both the employee of the board and the chief executive of the district. Without conscious, proactive effort, superintendents

---

*This is the first of many quotations from my interviews with board members. I have not provided
citations, and in some cases have altered wording slightly, so that I might honor my guarantee of
anonymity for individuals and for school districts.

can impede a board's understanding and execution of responsibility. Superintendents who want to efficiently accomplish their objectives or who fear board interference may not build board capacity to perform.

> The way the board operates depends a lot on the superintendent. We visit schools and go to functions; we're given ample communication and information.
>
> With elected boards, the superintendent should take the lead in looking with the board at how to be totally effective. He should get problems out in the open.
>
> We need to teach the board to stretch its thinking and to be thoughtful in selecting its leader. A leader can take a board many places. There's a need for training in understanding board leadership: how to maintain the board-administration partnership but take the board beyond where it is currently. The individual piece of this is, what can I as a board member do to address issues that I find important?

Boards complain: they are used as a rubber stamp for the superintendent; they are ignored; they have difficulty exercising their authority:

> The superintendent and assistant superintendent are a major frustration to me. The board is irrelevant as far as the administration is concerned. The administrators work around the board.
>
> The board usually goes along with the agenda of the superintendent unless someone questions an item; review is perfunctory unless triggered by specific concerns. There are usually two or three meetings each month. The superintendent runs the show.

The Role of the School Board

Many have written about school board responsibilities and the responsibilities of other boards of control.[3] At the core, a board has six primary responsibilities:

- It guides the accomplishment of the school district's purposes, particularly focused on the education of the district's children; it guides fundamental change in goals, programs, and structure.

- It screens and supports key projects identified to improve programs and operations, and it monitors progress to these ends; it also monitors the ongoing operation of the school district and its programs.

- It chooses, directs, and evaluates the superintendent of the district.

- It oversees the planning and deployment of resources, both material and human.

- It serves as a bridge between the district and the community, both in reflecting community desires and in promoting understanding and support; it leads the coalescing of disparate community views; it builds and maintains partnerships and collaborative relationships with other organizations.

- It ensures fiscal, legal, staff, and programmatic accountability.

The lack of clarity and the resulting misunderstanding of the board's role come about for two reasons: (1) the expectations of community and requirements of the state differ from board members' primary responsibilities; and (2) whether by choice, response to partisan pressure, or lack of understanding of responsibilities, board members spend time on less essential, or perhaps even incorrect, aspects of their work.

This misdirection of energy is often evident. One of our interviewees comments on micromanagement:

> One problem I faced was getting away from micromanaging the district. I got bogged down with little things: the politics, the hidden agendas. I learned that there are certain things you should do and certain things you shouldn't do. You have to see the whole picture. Then you can make better decisions.

Another board member talks about the diversion of conflict and personal agenda:

> One of the most frustrating parts of the job of board member is the conflict—conflict with the community, with the administration, and within the board itself. There's a need to separate the personal agenda from the bigger picture. A major problem is that if board members focus on a specific personal agenda, the administration may spend too much time on those areas.

The personal focus can be seductive, making clarity and perspective in the role of the board all the more difficult. As one board member says:

> Even though you get bogged down in little things, with everyone calling you, for me the satisfaction is helping individual parents with their problems.

Common Mistakes of School Boards

Given the difficult context within which boards function, and the difficulty they have in focusing on their primary responsibilities, boards, when they are unsuccessful, often make a handful of mistakes in the way they operate. Here (and summarized later in Exhibit I.1) are the six common ones that have the most telling consequences:

Mistake #1: Making political decisions.

School boards are in the business of making decisions. And decisions should be based on information, assessment of alternatives, and judgment. Uppermost on the agenda should be the questions, What actions are in the best interest of the children of the district? and Which of these can also gain public support?

However, board members often stand for election on a partisan basis. They may lack information and knowledge of alternative choices on issues under debate, and they can manipulate the decision-making process with hidden agendas and political alliances.

Some of the problems stem from the very reasons board members run for office. Many come to office with an agenda that, at least initially, politicizes decision making.

> I ran because I was concerned about the schools. I believe in public service and was approached by young parents—people unhappy with school board members who wanted a change. They were concerned about a number of specific issues, including abolishing the gifted program and the process by which the high school was closed.

With consistency, members cite similar concerns about their schools and school boards as reasons for seeking office. Other interviewees reflect on their interest in the power of the position:

> I'm a politician at heart and I care about kids.

Another said:

> The superintendent can be the most powerful person in the community. Running for the school board was a part of providing check and balance to that power.

Then there is the lack of information and alternatives—a situation that can work in favor of special interests and impede objective decision making. A typical comment:

> I find my work on the school board frustrating. There's lots of work, meetings, and reading. The frustrating part is there's no real control over anything. It's a struggle defining the role of the board. I'm not sure we're getting all the information. Solutions are presented and we're asked to give a yes or no answer. I have this feeling that I'm one of seven, that I don't really have influence. I want to contribute ideas but everything comes prepackaged.

Board members must use knowledge and ability to develop their own alternative proposals and demand, with assurance, information, and alternatives from the superintendent and staff.

Board members may politicize decision making. One board member talks about the lack of board trust:

> The most frustrating situations have been when I was deceived by other board members, where they represented situations as different from what they were.

Another talks about the frustration of hidden agendas. It's hard for board members to be effective in a politicized environment:

> As a new board member, functioning in the job is difficult. You are unsure about other people on the board. You want to find out their strengths and weaknesses before playing your hand. You don't want to be overly aggressive but want the board to know you are an equal member. The hardest part is finding out who has the information you want and what information exists.

Although many board elections are nonpartisan, politics plays a major role in school board activities. People have different agendas, often revealed behind the scenes. Decisions are made before they ever get to the board. Board effectiveness requires pushing personal agendas from center stage. Whenever school boards conduct their business with partisan judgment, they compromise their capacity to govern in the best interest of children and community.

Mistake #2: Functioning without ground rules.

School boards often conduct their business without reaching agreement on the fundamental rules that guide their actions. They do not resolve some basic issues: the relative roles of superintendent and board, the responsibilities of the board chair, the constraints on board members acting as individuals, the way information is requested and shared, their relationship with the media, the treatment of confidential information, public decorum, and respectful behavior. Disagreement about these actions undermines trust and mutual respect among board members and distracts them from substantive decision making.

On the board-administration relationship, one board member states:

> There's a need for board members to have rudimentary facts about the relationship between the administration and the board: how school board members work with each other and what they are entitled to expect from the superintendent. Consultants tell school board members how they should behave, but they come with a bias. School board members shouldn't be involved in personnel, but school boards can't wait for the superintendent in all situations. Members need to find their own conclusions. They should be exposed to a variety of perspectives about how the school board should conduct itself.

In one district, a board member reflects on the negative consequence of the lack of guidelines on shared information:

> I talked frequently with one board member. Then there was an incident in one of the schools. He said the faculty of the school didn't support a program. I found out he was misrepresenting the situation. I have come to see that you have to investigate situations yourself. You can't rely on other board members. You have to have your own broad range of constituents. You have to be an investigator.

Another board member discusses dysfunctional behavior by a board president:

> At times the board president has operated like a dictator. Perception of the board by the public can reflect the president's style. There should be a more open style; discipline is important but not like the army; there's a need for greater flexibility.

Here's a board comment on rules for public and private debate:

> The board is united in public and argues in private. Do we need to evaluate what we will get out of particular actions? My argument is we need to argue in public and to know what we're doing. It is effective if we have counterarguments in making decisions.

Another board member discusses differences in the way individual board members review administrative actions:

> I don't read administrative evaluations and only go into schools when I am invited. I put the responsibility on administrators to do this. Several other board members agree with my approach; others don't agree. They want to read evaluations.

Boards spend little time building consensus around their rules of operation. But time after time they cite their frustration over having to operate without consensus. They spend an inordinate amount of time discussing the problems created by the lack of systematic operational rules, building mutual distrust in the process. The net consequence is less effective attention to the real educational issues boards must address.

Mistake #3: Responding to coercion.

Boards function in a context of individuals and constituent groups, often at odds, and each with a strongly advocated agenda for board action. Although this can contribute to informed decision making, it too often results in distorted judgments based on the desire to appease a particular constituency rather than the need to do what is best for all children.

Here's an example illustrating the difficulty of separating informed decision making from coercion:

> We had a number of new administrators. In one building, there were many things reported to be going on that weren't going on. There were two factions—25 percent who were very happy and 75 percent who were not happy. The board was also split about the situation. We had to decide whether to get rid of the principal.

Another example shows the political difficulty of determining the objective response.

> We had a case involving a student who was an outstanding athlete. In the beginning of his junior year, just before basketball season started, a girl gave him a "box cutter" to hold for her. The administration was tipped off. The hearing officer recommended expulsion in accordance with policy. The community, 350 strong, came to the meeting in support of keeping the student in school. The board voted to overrule the hearing examiner.

Coercion can also come from the superintendent and administration:

> The board was in the middle of discussing raising graduation requirements and setting requirements for participation in extracurricular activities when I joined the board. There were four votes to change the policy, and they didn't waffle in the face of passionate administrative "pitch" not to make the policy changes. The administration said it would destroy kids if they got behind and couldn't participate in extracurricular activities.

Distinguishing between coercion and objective judgment is not easy when the superintendent is stating his or her professional opinion of educational policy.

Boards must be responsive to community concern; they must carefully consider the professional judgment of their superintendent. Yet it is always a mistake to allow the community or superintendent to force judgments not based on student welfare.

Mistake #4: Not connecting with the community.

Boards sometimes function without connecting with the community they serve. They may not provide information or solicit input; they may provide inadequate opportunity for dialogue. They structure meetings so the community does not see the full board discussion.

As a consequence they operate without full information, lose the opportunity to build community trust in the board decision-making process, and fail to build community understanding of the basis for their decisions.

Often this failure to connect becomes the impetus for candidates to run for board office:

> Before I became a board member, I attended public sessions of the board for almost two years. It taught me almost nothing. The public sessions of the board are so carefully choreographed. The leadership of a board can design public meetings to minimize public confrontation, almost negating public commitment. You end up with civil and boring board meetings.
>
> We are trying to avoid the major mistake of letting the perception continue that community input is not important. We are starting to do something by confronting the situation and contacting those with concerns. We need to respond with correct information.

Sometimes, despite the best intentions, the distasteful dialogue with strong opponents acts as a disincentive to full connection with community:

There are certain elements of working through controversy with the community that are very negative. There are those who fight the board, who sue the board. There's a group that's unwilling to accept our decision.

The biggest mistake we have made in the past was not dealing with the public as they really exist. If you keep information from the public or don't deal with issues head on, it creates problems. For example, it took us eight years to acknowledge the racial balance issue. Now we don't let things get too far before we deal with them. We don't stop talking until the issue is resolved.

In Delaware and elsewhere, there are certain issues, such as capital expenditures, that may require a public referendum, providing an incentive to foster good community relations:

We have a capital referendum coming up this year. The priority last fall was to improve community relations to assure passage of the referendum. There's a vocal negative group. We had a meeting with this group. Their primary concern was that "no one listens to us."

Whether it's willful or out of neglect, when boards don't fully connect with their communities, they disregard a primary responsibility and seriously cripple their effectiveness.

Mistake #5: Neglecting self-improvement.

Board members learn how to do their job by doing it and through informal, ad hoc conversation with board members and the superintendent. Yet they begin their work with little previous experience, and it often takes two years to learn the basic job. Even then, there are continuing challenges to their competence. The result is unpredictable, uneven performance and an on-the-job education in which members learn from their mistakes.

Board members remember the feeling of being overwhelmed and scared. Most emphasize the informal process. Board improvement is "bootstrap," that is, see what works and what doesn't. They cite the lack of training:

We're not good at orienting new board members. It takes a long time to learn about the board. I learn every day from fellow board members.

There's a need to bring new board members up to speed. It takes twelve to eighteen months. There's a need to have a training program at the beginning for new board members to help them understand budgeting, finance, planning, and so forth.

They emphasize the continuing need for discussion on broader issues and operational rules:

> The board needs time with staff to work on expectations for children—time to talk about the big philosophical picture. We don't have retreats. They are not discussed. We were taken to court for violation of the sunshine law and the retreats were stopped. The administrators have a retreat and the board comes for a portion of it. The board needs to do more.

Yet when opportunities are presented, board members feel the constraints of time and money and often decline training or self-improvement opportunities. Thus the capacity for effective boardsmanship is not fully realized.

Mistake #6: Taking fragmented actions.

Boards experience problems when they consider each issue as a separate item rather than prioritizing based on the issue's contribution to overall objectives. New board members focus on the specific issues that brought them to office. Distrust of the superintendent and a variety of complaints from the community lead to a focus on detailed management issues. The sum is a mosaic without pattern or relief; the important district direction is lost in conflicting or unrelated minor initiatives.

Board elections often focus on specific issues. The gifted program and family life curriculum are prime examples. Waste in spending, financial management, building construction, school closings, the quality of public involvement, lack of student discipline, and desegregation plans also garner lots of election-year attention. New board members then come onto the board with a background and interest in single issues or single schools:

> One problem I faced was getting away from micromanaging the district. I got bogged down with little things: the politics, the hidden agendas. I learned that there are certain things you should do and certain things you shouldn't do. You have to see the whole picture. Then you can make better decisions.

With its focus on specific decisions, the board work reinforces fragmentation. Board members see the narrowness of this approach.

> There is a need for more opportunity to discuss values, concerns, issues, and not just decisions.

There is a need for more self-initiative by the board. More things could happen if the board was a proactive partner. We need to be asking where we are headed and to represent the community interest. We need to be independent and not rely solely on our infrastructure. We need to fulfill the trustee-ship role.

But some board members are simply focused on their own agenda:

One of the board members is outspoken and an advocate of a particular viewpoint. He played to the parents and lobbied for his viewpoint. He wasn't trying to look at what's best in the long term.

The array of independent decisions, however important, does not provide the vision and strategy necessary for leadership or change.

How to Build the Capacity to Govern

Critics of school boards believe these boards do not contribute to the systemic change required if our nation's children are to be well educated. They want educational excellence for all children. They expect progress toward a vision of the future that strengthens academic skills and other student competencies. They want accountability for the effectiveness and productivity of school district employees. And they want boards to form an effective bridge between community and school district—one that enables the district to understand community desires and the community to understand the district's work.

Most of us agree that these are central objectives and that school board leadership is essential to their realization. But we don't always agree on the changes necessary to achieve these objectives. That debate continues.

In my view it is, at its core, a question of capacity, not of direction. The six mistakes school boards make involve the process by which they do their work, not the particular policies they recommend. School boards must build their capacity to govern, whatever the policy.

Our leaders and educational experts must help school boards, not by guiding them in policy matters (although that guidance will always be helpful) but by building their capacity to achieve these objectives for their communities. Furthermore, both the superintendent and the community leadership can contribute to this capacity building. Boards must tap this resource.

See Exhibit I.1 for a recap of what boards often do wrong.

EXHIBIT I.1

Six Common Mistakes That School Boards Make

1. MAKE POLITICAL DECISIONS

Boards make decisions that are not based on objective information, assessment of alternatives, and rational judgment but have a partisan bias that supports hidden agendas and political alliances.

2. FUNCTION WITHOUT GROUND RULES

Boards conduct business without agreement on fundamental rules concerning the relative roles of superintendent and board, the responsibilities of the board chair, the constraints on individual board action, and the use of information and public decorum. Disagreement about these actions undermines trust and mutual respect.

3. RESPOND TO COERCION

Boards allow particular constituencies, instead of what is best for all children, to influence their decisions.

4. FAIL TO CONNECT WITH COMMUNITY

Boards do not provide information to the community; they fail to solicit input and offer inadequate opportunity for dialogue—all leading to community distrust and lack of understanding.

5. NEGLECT SELF-IMPROVEMENT

Board members do not seek out self-improvement opportunities, and their performance is uneven and unpredictable.

6. TAKE FRAGMENTED ACTIONS

Boards consider each issue as a separate item without priority; important district direction is lost in conflicting or unrelated minor initiatives.

Part One

A Model for Board Effectiveness

Chapter 1

Making Rational Decisions

DECISION MAKING is the lifeblood of a school board. Boards have power and authority over a range of topics, and with this power goes the obligation to make the best decisions possible. It is no surprise that when board members are asked what makes them effective, they talk about the way they decide things, from virtually automatic appointments to potentially divisive issues.

Boards describe a rational, informed decision-making process in which they consider the merits of alternative courses of action. One board member says:

> I define board effectiveness as directly related to the board's role as a policymaking body. The issue of the desegregation appeal was just such a policy initiative expressing the district's philosophy regarding diversity. There was discussion about establishing percentages. The board had different and stronger views for diversity than the state legislators. The board did its homework, got statistics, got background from staff, framed choices based on what was realistic.
>
> When the court order was lifted, there was a need to have things in place for charter and choice. The superintendent brought his experience. Some board members had done personal research. The majority of board members understood and valued diversity. The administration prepared the numbers and the "what-if" scenarios. There were seven to eight board meetings and one or two work sessions over the two-month period. The administration brought information. The idea was to let the board decide rather than "telling the board" what to do. We agreed we needed to work closely together. There was one

"loose cannon" on the board. The president had that board member sit next to him and tried to control the grandstanding. The president talked with the board member, trying to find out major concerns. The idea was to coach for good boardsmanship.

We had a candid discussion of diversity. Two board members are minorities and they're especially concerned about resegregation. The issue was how to keep cool heads. Some board members needed defusing. We used humor and avoided embarrassing individual board members.

What was good about this situation was that we made our decision backed by solid information and data. It was not a gut response. We tried to get as much information as possible. We didn't act out of personal emotions. We focused on the substance of the issue, not on political alliances.

In candid remarks such as these, board members describe the importance of making substantive, rational decisions rather than making them for emotional or political reasons. Getting to that point requires a decision-making process that exhibits distinctive characteristics. Analysis of the interviews with board members shows four factors that are cited repeatedly as indicators of boards acting effectively in making the countless decisions members face during their terms. The data show that boards are most effective when they can

Access and use relevant information

Discuss deliberately

Consider alternative actions

Work toward consensus

1. Access and Use Relevant Information

Relevant information comes from multiple sources, including district staff and community; it is focused on central board concerns such as resolving immediate crises and strengthening longer-term educational results; it is accurate, balanced, and presented as an efficient guide for action.

Information is critical to decision making. It provides the context for objective, rational action. It can present alternatives and the logical reasoning behind them. It provides insight into constituent perceptions. When fully shared, information gives board members the same basis for considering issues.

One board member discusses the critical importance of obtaining input from a variety of sources, especially during such volatile issues as student reassignments:

> We transferred ninety-two students from one middle school to another. The superintendent provided all kinds of data with alternatives. A community group disagreed with the board. It included eight to ten people, including one board member. Five hours of public input went into the process. We reached a decision based on objective criteria.
>
> We were effective because our decision was information-based and included lots of public input. There was lots of discussion of pros and cons and alternatives.

Describing the same situation, another board member notes the importance of getting technical information from the superintendent and district staff:

> The superintendent came to the board suggesting several ways to solve the overcrowding problem. The board looked at several solutions [and] . . . was open and honest in the process, willing to listen. It's OK to disagree. There is respect. Board members listen to the rationale and opinions of others. The district did studies and provided us with information on the number of rooms, the number of students and teaching units. The district did test runs regarding distance and time. Then there was discussion explaining where the board stood—the need for transfers and the problems with the other options.
>
> The board had support for its work through the team of the superintendent, the finance director, and other staff. We were able to get answers to our questions—not the answers they thought we wanted to hear but the best answers.

Many of those interviewed reaffirm the obvious need for information in such areas as personnel:

> The superintendent evaluation process was put in the superintendent's contract. This spring, the board had three sessions to collect and collate information and provide the superintendent with feedback.

And the need for budgeting is affirmed:

> There is tremendous credibility between the board and district personnel. We always get the rationale for why decisions are made.

2. Discuss Deliberately

Deliberate discussions leading to board decisions are systematic, objective, and open; board members frame issues, consider information and context, and give the time necessary to avoid forcing decisions prematurely; they put aside personal differences, lack hidden agendas, and consider without prejudice the merits of the particular situation or issue; they are honest and forthright in their exchange of viewpoints.

Such deliberative activity includes questioning administrative recommendations before accepting or rejecting them. Discussions reveal the desire of board members to understand the issues at hand.

In cases cited by the interviewees as examples of board effectiveness, deliberative discussion exhibited multiple characteristics, including sufficient time, planning, and the extra effort to review facts and expert opinion if needed. Here is just one example of such a deliberate process:

> There was the consent order in late 1993. The judge thought the districts could reach agreement. For two months the board conducted workshops. We sat down and discussed each point in the consent order. We asked for public comment. We took the order apart piece by piece. We took time. We were analytical. We came to agreement about the action. We didn't allow petty things to enter in. We were able to come to terms, and this was tough; we are seven people with different backgrounds.

There are many other examples. Discussing the planning process, one board member involved in a superintendent search states:

> We involved staff, community, and board in the process. We narrowed it to three candidates and sent people to visit them. We chose one of the three and he turned us down. In beginning of this process, we had to decide what we wanted to accomplish in the next five years. Did we want the best in the state, a person known regionally as superlative, or a person known nationally as exceptional? We were united and adamant in

wanting the best nationally. This was reaffirmed as we conducted a new search.

Throughout our work, the board kept the welfare of our children as the paramount goal. We were able to articulate what we wanted in a superintendent and were unwilling to settle for less. Our approach was honest. When we went back to go through the process again, we asked what we should change. People said they liked it the way it was.

Another speaks in detail about the timing of the budget process, illustrating board effectiveness through a step-by-step description of decision making about the budget:

It's an ongoing activity. We approve it in August and make amendments in February. Information is accessible. Once a month there's a public review of revenues and expenses. We look at the numbers several times a year at meetings and workshops. Twice a year we present the budget at public hearings. It's an open process.

In another instance, an interviewee speaks of the board taking the initiative, against the superintendent's recommendation, to hold a hearing concerning teacher layoffs and tenure:

The board members opted for the hearings to make sure the information they had about the teacher's situation was correct. There was an uproar about the superintendent's position, complaints from staff and parents, and the board felt it should respond. In some instances, the board overturned the superintendent's layoff decisions. The board was sending a message that it is willing to be fair and open-minded.

In another example of an effective decision-making process cited in the interviews, health professionals offered expert opinion about a controversial proposal to create a school wellness center:

Some critics asked whether we were condoning sex and giving out contraceptives. There was lots of hot discussion with parents for and against. We agreed that parents would sign an authorization for their children to use the center. We had medical doctors and others from the health community speak. The administration advocated the center and the board finally voted 5-2 for approval. Now we have one in each high school.

A number of the interviewees link the effectiveness of specific board actions with the board's ability to objectively examine important issues. One interviewee speaks of an administrative contract renewal decision based on the merits of the case. Another cites the board's ability to discuss differences rationally and to disagree without personal attacks. Yet another board member describes his board's focus on the substance of the issue, not on political alliances. Finally, an appointed member of a vocational board suggests that there are no special interests because his board is appointed, not elected:

> This situation was to determine what to do with one of our schools. The entranceway was pathetic. What can we do about it? Put in a new entrance with 60/40 money from the state. Why was this an example of board effectiveness? I was the new person coming on the board. Other board members were willing to look at the idea. They were listening and respecting the views of others. The board, on most every occasion, is willing to consider ideas; there are no cliques; no special interests. There is not a member on this board who would run for election. With elected boards, board members often have specific interests.

Many interviewees point to the openness of their board as an essential ingredient in deliberate decision making. "Conducting open and honest dialogue" and "stepping up to the plate and sharing their views" are representative observations within the situations cited as examples of effectiveness. Here's an example:

> We are in the final stages of a superintendent search. The current superintendent, who's retiring, has been in the district since 1970 and superintendent since 1989. He is well liked and respected. We began the process by getting input from faculty, parents, and community members, identifying the traits and characteristics they wanted in a new superintendent. This helped us focus on what kind of person they wanted: a top-down curriculum person—a people person who can lead shared decision making and work with groups.
>
> The process has included advertising, initial interviews, and final interviews. We now have two good people to decide between.

3. Consider Alternative Actions

Consideration of alternative actions indicates that the discussion reflects different points of view, hears all sides, and assesses the positive and negative consequences of various choices.

Interviewees highlight the importance of considering alternatives in effective decision making. These tend to be highly visible situations that spark strong community viewpoints: superintendent searches, the redistricting of schools, and desegregation. In the first example, viable alternatives put before the board allow for effective decision making—for the working through of divergent opinions to reach consensus:

> There was a superintendent search after the previous superintendent decided not to serve. The board contacted a number of sources, including the National School Boards Association (NSBA) and consultants. A consultant helped facilitate the process through initial paper screening and interviews. The board did its own interviews when the field was narrowed to fifteen. The superintendent was chosen from three finalists.
>
> At the time there was a divergence of opinion. The board was able to come together to reach consensus. Because it was a personnel matter, it could be discussed out of the sunshine. This allowed for a frank discussion of differences. There was the realization by the board that they had to find a new superintendent and needed to put aside personal agendas to do so.

In the second example, the alternatives again set the stage for effective decision making. This time the superintendent comes to the board with several options, a technique suggested in many cases:

> We had a situation where there was a need to redraw the district lines because some schools had more students. The staff ran hearings. These were public meetings. We received lots of input from parents. Board members could go if they wanted to but they didn't have to. The staff looked carefully at the situation . . . at the shortest routes to specific schools and the number of kids who fit. The board then looked at different alternative plans. The board and administrative jobs were distinct.
>
> This was an example of board effectiveness because no board member had a hidden agenda. No one was trying to be political. Everyone was trying to do right by all the children.

We ironed out differences in executive session and presented a united perspective in public. What I liked about the board's action was that each of us represented all children and not a particular group of constituents.

4. Work Toward Consensus

When boards work toward consensus, board members try to find areas of commonality; they tolerate ambiguity and recognize the need for compromise and the importance of reaching agreement.

Board members emphasize the importance of building consensus for their decisions—and for good reason. The board has the responsibility of finding a common base of community support for the school district and its programs. It reflects this responsibility as it seeks consensus. Furthermore, the board has the authority to act as an entity, not a collection of board members. Once a decision is made, the leadership and integrity of that action is best transmitted without the distraction of opposing positions. Consensus building enhances community support and channels controversy toward reaching support for constructive action.

Board interviews reflect this rationale. For example, in one situation there was a highly sensitive personnel issue:

> The board stayed together as a unit. Only one board member spoke to the newspaper. He said something inaccurate; the others said "no comment." The board kept control and reached an effective decision. The board members listened to each other. People stated their own opinions. This illustrates the board working together as a unit, not as individuals, supporting each other, protecting the employee. There was consensus to protect the individual, but also the district.

Here the board was conscious of providing a public image of consensus. In a sensitive situation, the board wanted to demonstrate by its actions that it supported the decision it had made. In other situations, consensus requires compromise, that is, the recognition that the board must live with and support a decision of the majority, even when it is a controversial matter such as redistricting:

> Everyone had to give. It was not a unanimous decision. Everyone agreed something had to be done. Board members were able to say, this isn't my first choice but I'll abide by it. They

respected the vote of the majority and supported what the children needed.

Often, interviewees refer to successful consensus building around shared assumptions that will underlie the eventual decision. In a superintendent search, one school board member says:

> It was a good consensus-building effort. We started talking about what we were looking for. We wanted the best; we wanted to be the top. That has driven everything since then. We have agreed that we needed to do what's best for all students in the district. We have operated like a big family. We have had our differences; we've each voiced our opinions; people have agreed or disagreed. But once the vote is taken, everyone gets behind a decision. This is less true now because there is a single-issue board member. The board represents a mix of personalities with diverse backgrounds. Many went to high school together. We have worked hard to consider all three communities served by the district.

All the examples weren't positive, and the consensus-seeking process is fragile; it can be disrupted if a single board member doesn't buy into the approach. In one case involving a feeder pattern, the interviewee states:

> It was a controversial decision. The board made the decision 4-3. The community tried to fight. A new board member was sniping about the decision. An effective board respects the decision of the majority; this board member doesn't.

Part of consensus building is seeking an approach that can gain broad support. Here the flexibility to use alternative approaches to fulfill a board objective becomes important. In this example, a board adjusted in the context of community pressure and board member vacillation to achieve an ultimate direction:

> There was a confrontation with a minority group. It was volatile and ugly, with threats of violence. We met with people; we let them say how they felt. We compromised and avoided an ugly problem. We figured a way to work it out. We were going to let a certain administrator go and the group didn't want this. The president and the superintendent conferred. They thought a meeting would be a good idea. They consulted with each board member to ask if that was okay. After the

meeting, some board members backtracked; they said we shouldn't proceed. So we let it go. Then we got a new superintendent. He addressed the problem with a new strategic plan. This demonstrated our effectiveness because we listened to the community and were able to relate to the community. We were able to step back, look at the situation, and start over again. Everyone supported the decision to step back. The essential ingredient was that we had people on the board who were willing to compromise.

Exhibit 1.1 summarizes the components of good decision making.

 ## What Boards Can Do

Board comments confirm a common wisdom about board decision making—wisdom that isn't always honored in practice. In the heat of a discussion

---

EXHIBIT 1.1
Elements of Effective Decision Making

ACCESS AND USE RELEVANT INFORMATION
Relevant information comes from many sources, including district staff and community; it is focused on central board concerns: resolving immediate crises and strengthening longer-term educational results; it is accurate, balanced, and presented as an efficient guide for action.

DISCUSS ISSUES DELIBERATELY
Deliberate discussions leading to board decisions are systematic, objective, and open; board members frame issues, consider information and context, and give the time necessary to avoid forcing decisions prematurely. They put aside personal differences, lack hidden agendas, and consider without prejudice the merits of the particular situation or issue, and are honest and forthright in their exchange of viewpoints.

CONSIDER ALTERNATIVE ACTIONS
Consideration of alternative actions indicates that the discussion reflects different points of view, hears all sides, and assesses the positive and negative consequences of various choices.

WORK TOWARD CONSENSUS
When boards work toward consensus, board members try to find areas of commonality, tolerate ambiguity, and recognize the need for compromise and the importance of reaching agreement.

it's not easy to apply the rules consistently. Here are four action steps that may help:

1. *Build integrity into the process.* Board members should agree on the way decisions are made and should monitor, enforce, and publicize agreements they make. The process is analytical, informed by the facts surrounding an issue, alternative resolutions, rationale, experience, and public perception. The process is also open and deliberate; it is subject to schedules and timing but not aborted prematurely, despite pressure for action. Board members should continually monitor and critique their actions to give integrity to the process.

2. *Reach agreement even without consensus.* No matter how careful the process, it's not possible to reach consensus on every issue. It is possible, however, to agree that the problem deserves a solution. What is tricky is the way in which the board presents its support. When boards split on difficult issues, with members explaining their rationales for positive and negative votes, I am always impressed when the spirit of discussion and presentation demonstrates respect for the process and commitment to implement the action approved.

3. *Rely on the superintendent.* The superintendent is key to the process, providing most of the information and crafting alternative recommendations for board approval. Boards should expect superintendents to be factual, to objectively provide relevant information, and to facilitate the decision process. The board must be prepared to seek information elsewhere and to fashion its own alternatives if the superintendent doesn't provide the needed support. The board must strike a balance between holding the superintendent strictly accountable for high-quality support and tolerating the inevitable slippage that occurs with the demands on the superintendency. But if the lack of support forms a pattern, it's time to look for a new superintendent. It's that important!

4. *Encourage public involvement—without capitulation.* Boards encourage public input and invest energy in understanding community perspectives. When things get tough, boards may run for cover or yield to pressure. Neither action supports school board effectiveness. Boards should guard against the overuse of executive session or individual, private communications to reach consensus. This subverts the public understanding of the process of weighing alternative actions.

Although it's not easy, the decision process must be objective, not based on political consequences. Here's an example of a board working hard to achieve that balance:

The state offered us dollars to provide a wellness center in the schools. One board member was adamantly opposed and very vocal. One board member was supportive. There were a lot of hearings. There was an extremely vocal group adamantly opposed. There were moral issues and tax issues. Board members attended hearings. The board did a good job of investigation, polling the community. A problem in the past was that the board was accused of not caring what the community thinks. I went to the Department of Health and got answers in writing, where there were questions about the parameters of the center. We approved the center and put opponents on the committee overseeing its operation.

Exhibit 1.2 provides questions for you to consider when trying to determine whether your board's decision-making process is sound.

EXHIBIT 1.2

Questions to Consider

Does your board work to reach consensus on important matters?

Is your board aware of the subtleties of the issues it considers?

Does your board explicitly examine the "downside" or possible pitfalls of any important decision it is about to make?

Does your board see issues as related to one another?

Do the decisions of your board on one issue tend to influence what you do about other issues that come before you?

Do your board's decisions usually result in a split vote?

When faced with an important issue, does your board often "brainstorm" and try to generate a list of creative approaches or solutions?

Does a certain group of board members usually vote together (for or against) on particular issues?

Does your board often request postponement of a decision until further information can be obtained?

Does your board usually receive a full rationale for the recommendations it is asked to act upon?

Does your board try to avoid ambiguous and complicated issues?

Does your board spend a lot of time listening to different points of view before it votes on an important matter?

Do all board members support majority decisions?

Chapter 2

Functioning Cohesively as a Group

A HEALTHY DECISION-MAKING PROCESS naturally flows from board members working together to fulfill their responsibilities. When school board members gel as a unit, they exhibit many characteristics of other well-functioning groups: a shared respect and trust that recognizes the contribution of each individual, a feeling of cohesiveness, shared goals for the board, able leadership within the board (often the board president), shared values, and agreement on the board's operating rules.

The importance of school board responsibilities and the limited time and experience of individual board members make effective functioning as a group all the more important. Boards must guide district purposes and plans, oversee distribution of resources, and provide accountability to community and state government while mediating controversy. Legally, it is the board, not individual members, that is empowered to act. Thus the ability of individual board members to function as a group becomes a critical element in the effective operation of school boards.

The importance of these characteristics of group function becomes particularly evident when board members face trying times.

> In the mid-80s, the school district was overrun with controversy. The court was mandating assignments, and the schools were getting poorer academically. There was political in-fighting. I believed the problem was in the way in which students were assigned. Meetings were vicious. There was a lack of trust. Easy items were made hard. There was partisan nastiness, with the board splitting votes 4-3.
>
> Trust was the most important ingredient needed. This comes from participation in governance. How people feel about the schools has implications for how good the schools are. The

board built a bond over the years. Members tried hard to work with each other. This led to a plan of action to return confidence to the board. In 1992 we agreed that at the high school we would work toward a choice plan. What helped bring this about? Some board members left the board. I became president. I knew we had to work better together but we couldn't compromise on the clear path. These were people of good faith. The superintendent and I did some planning as to how we could shape proposals to the board. The superintendent never worked against the vision, but it never would have gotten there without board leadership. Getting the proposals approved required rational planning and strategizing. School boards become important when times are tough and resolution is necessary. You need to have a way of resolving difficulties.

During interviews board members identified five primary activities that play an essential role in a board's functioning effectively as a group. Analysis of their responses indicates that boards come together well as a group when they

Operate with norms

Demonstrate leadership

Articulate cohesiveness

Act on values

Show respect

1. Operate with Norms

Board members share an agreement or understanding about certain aspects of the way they will operate. Some of the most common norms are summarized in Exhibit 2.1.

Decide by consensus and give unanimous support.

The board settles differences of opinion by discussion to reach consensus, not by vote. Each board member honors a board decision as an action that requires unanimous support.

In many cases, boards agree on a course of action and are committed to carrying it out. As one board member states: "Board members were willing to disagree, but once settled, they supported the decision." Another says: "The board was able to accept the majority vote as the will of the board."

EXHIBIT 2.1
Common Norms for Board Operations

MAKE DECISIONS BY CONSENSUS

Wherever possible, the board tries to settle differences of opinion by discussion before voting.

SUPPORT DECISIONS UNANIMOUSLY

Board members, respecting the board's authority to act as a unit, support board decisions, whatever the member's own views might be.

DISCUSS ISSUES PUBLICLY

The board, whatever private discourse precedes, ensures that full discussion of issues takes place in public prior to a vote. The board members work out routines to explore viewpoints privately and legally in preparation for public discussion.

HONOR CONFIDENTIALITY

Board members maintain confidentiality where appropriate, particularly with regard to information about personnel decisions, other actions protected from open disclosure, and specific off-the-record interactions among board members.

PARTICIPATE WITH COMMITMENT

Board members invest the time and effort to review materials and participate in meetings.

SET THE AGENDA

The board president and superintendent jointly set the board agenda with input from other members.

CONTACT STAFF AND VISIT SCHOOLS APPROPRIATELY

A process is established and followed by each board member to ensure that schools are not disrupted, that the superintendent is aware of board presence in schools, and that information is shared among board members as it relates to board decision making.

One interviewee emphasizes the importance of board president leadership in achieving the norm of consensus:

> The president is responsible for building consensus. There is a need to be open and honest and above board, not to pit one board member against another . . . to be knowledgeable . . . get a feeling for how particular board members think. Answer questions to get them to go along with the others; figure out what hang-ups they have.

Prepare and provide for public discussion.

The use of public sessions is deliberate in preserving open discussion of all issues not protected by law. Executive sessions, when permitted, provide opportunities for private exploration of individual board member viewpoints that provide perspective to that discussion. The superintendent, president of the board, and other members engage in one-on-one private conversations in advance of board meetings to gauge the level of support for proposals and to help formulate compromises that have board support, while not compromising the spirit or letter of open public discussion.

In many cases informal, individual talks precede formal board discussion. For example, where a board was concerned about a superintendent's performance, one interviewee recounts: "Board members had telephone conversations that things were not going well. We had an executive session without the superintendent." Another interviewee, answering how it was possible to reach consensus on a controversial issue, explains: "What makes it work is that individual board members and the board president talk to see how people feel. Then we had an executive session meeting."

Then there is the question of how business is discussed during an executive versus a public session. As one board member puts it: "We ironed out differences in executive session and presented a united perspective in public." Another board member states: "The discussion in executive session was not carried over to public session. On certain topics concerning personnel and student personnel, as well as facilities, finance, and litigation, these discussions are perfectly legal and, in analyzing members' interviews, often preferred by boards who see 'out-of-the sunshine' discussions as contributing to board effectiveness." For example:

> At the time there was a divergence of opinion. The board was able to come together to reach consensus. Because it was a personnel matter, it could be discussed out of the sunshine. This allowed for a frank discussion of differences. There was the realization by the board that they had to find a new superintendent and needed to put aside personal agendas to do so.

In another case involving student expulsions, an interviewee states:

> We will often spend two hours on one such case. Each board member brings a different perspective to our discussion. It's necessary to have four votes to take action. I feel the need to support the expulsions and get the vote. In executive session, the total board discusses the action needed.

This illustrates board effectiveness in a number of ways. Each board member is involved in reading the transcript of the hearing. Each board member contributes some thought to the discussion. All make comments. Usually, the final decision is unanimous. We talk about it at length in executive session, then go to the public session and vote.

Board comments illustrate the sensitive balance between the opportunity for private, forthright discussion and the need for public debate and full disclosure. Board members see lively, even heated public debate as serving a legitimate purpose. In the context of a decision-making process on desegregation, one member says:

> We were willing to step forward to take the heat. We dealt with things in public; we didn't talk behind closed doors. We knew you can't deal privately with this kind of issue and get anywhere. We built trust with the community.

Another interviewee comments on board behavior, which, although leading to efficient operation, could arouse negative public reaction: "Often board meetings look cut and dry because considerable discussion has already occurred."

Honor confidentiality.

The board members protect each other and staff in maintaining confidentiality, especially with regard to information about personnel decisions, other actions protected from open disclosure, and specific off-the-record interactions among board members.

For example, one board member, discussing the board working together, recalls the controversial transfer of an administrator:

> The superintendent kept the board apprised of this situation, and the transfer was accomplished last year. The board hung together on this. The two new board members were given the personnel record of this administrator and didn't violate confidentiality. There was a lot of heat from a group of people about the decision to transfer, but because it was a personnel decision, the board couldn't talk about it. The board held together because members believe that doing the right thing is what counts.

Participate with commitment.

Board members invest the time and effort to review materials and participate in meetings. As one board member comments about teacher contract negotiations:

> The board worked together on this. The financial part was difficult. Board members had to build an understanding of finances and their own budget. No one was grandstanding. Ultimately, the effectiveness was due to people doing their homework, spending time with each other to be sure that issues were discussed and all understood.

Set an agenda.

The board president and superintendent jointly set the board agenda with input from other members.

Many board members comment on agenda setting and its central influence on the quality of the working relationship between board and superintendent. One board member comments critically:

> The board usually goes along with the agenda of the superintendent unless someone questions an item; review is perfunctory unless triggered by specific concerns. The superintendent runs the show.

Another is critical of the dominant role of president:

> The board operates with strong leadership from the president and vice president. They run a tight ship. We move quickly from one issue to the next to eliminate disagreement. The president is in the central office almost every day.

A commentary from one board member captures the spirit of most board discussion of agenda setting:

> The relationship between the board and superintendent depends upon who is strong and who is weak. The president of the board has the responsibility to "tee" questions up for the board, to be sure the board has information, the issues have been framed, and that they won't be blindsided politically. The president must develop a ritual and figurative agenda that is critical to board functioning. There is dysfunction on the board when the board members are surprised or uninformed. A strong superintendent is savvy. He knows where he wants to go and how to make the board comfortable.

Contact staff and visit schools as appropriate.

There are rules governing the way an individual board member may request information and discuss issues with staff and visit schools. Districts vary with respect to these rules, and board members see them as important to effective functioning. One board member commends his board's approach:

> Open style, consensus-building process, very few 4-3 votes. The board tries to build unanimity. There is a free flow of information. Anyone can ask a question at any time. Board members can ask anyone—any staff member who can give the best answer. The board expects straight answers. This sets the tone and direction for the district.

Another board member emphasizes the formality of their process:

> There are written guidelines for the board. All information requests go to the superintendent. We can visit the schools but must advise as to whether we are visiting as board member, citizen, or parent.

One board member laments a restrictive policy:

> I have difficulty with the rule that we should stay out of the schools. A board member will visit a school and go back to the administration asking why we are doing things as we are. The superintendent says the information obtained by the board member can't be used in discussion by the board.

But the involvement of board members in school visits and talking with staff is a delicate issue, open to abuse. In one case:

> Two school board members believe one other member is using his position to gain advantage for his child in school. The child was involved in a cheating scandal; the school board member approached the teacher and the problem went away.

In another, more ambiguous case:

> There was a new building administrator in one building. There were many things reported to be going on that weren't going on. There were two factions [of parents]. The board had also split about the situation. The board [and superintendent]

visited the school, talked with faculty, listened to different points of view, and made a decision on the administrator's contract.

This case illustrates the importance of rules and the difficulty of certain situations. Visits to schools or discussions with staff may be critically important but have an impact on the boundary between superintendent and board responsibilities. Board members need the insight provided by direct staff conversation, and staff are often encouraged by board interest and attention. However, a board member's involvement with staff can slip into attempts to influence school management, undermining the principal's authority and abusing the board's authority, which is collective, not individual.

The interviews also illustrate the way norms evolve in most districts. They are informal understandings, fashioned out of necessity in particular situations, dependent upon superintendent, board president, or other board members assuming leadership in developing and enforcing them. The more systematic and formal the development and enforcement process, the more likely they are to work.

2. Demonstrate Leadership

The board shows clear evidence of leadership. Usually, but not always, the board president takes the lead. In many instances, individual members will exercise leadership in particular situations. This leadership has many forms, including

Facilitating: encouraging and enabling efficient and effective board action

Representing: acting for the board in maintaining the board-superintendent working relationship

Informing: ensuring the flow of information from the district to the board to guarantee that each board member has equal access to appropriate information

Directing: providing the vision to assist the board in developing common goals for district improvement; proposing strategies the board could employ for achieving these goals

This leadership does not refer to the broad district leadership required of superintendent and board in partnership. Leading the district in achieving its goals and meeting standards is a subject for another time. Here, board leadership refers to the more narrow but equally important actions necessary for the board to function as a group.

The ability to defuse potentially explosive discussions, either among board members or between the board and community or staff, proves invaluable in a leader. It is critical to facilitating efficient and effective group functioning. In one instance, the president takes on this role:

> By focusing on the problem, the issue did not escalate. The meeting enabled each board member to hear the information first hand. The board president emphasized that consensus was important.

As in the case just described, leadership proves critical, especially when the inevitable bureaucratic mishaps occur:

> The board missed a deadline for a newspaper advertisement of a referendum. The district stood to lose $85 million as a consequence. The superintendent called the board president and agreed to call a board meeting. The superintendent called each member of the board. The situation could have resulted in name-calling. The board was asked to focus on the issue not on personnel. The meeting was held excluding the superintendent and other staff. The board president just focused on what should happen. He kept from laying blame . . . and the issue did not escalate.

And in another tense situation:

> We had to determine whether the board would approve the consent decree approved by the state. Each of the local boards involved agreed to vote on the same night. The president of the board prolonged the debate in executive session. This changed the polling of the board to a 4-3 vote to support the decree. She would not go into public session until we had a vote approving.

3. Articulate Cohesiveness

The board consciously expresses its common group mission. It becomes clear to the board, district staff, and the public that the board is working together to achieve common ends.

In many instances, board members talk about the board as a cohesive group and about importance of this in their effectiveness. Members use such words as *family* and *camaraderie* when describing their relationships with each other. One board member speaks of putting aside personal agendas, and yet another cites the importance of the board working as a whole, not as individuals. For example:

> We reviewed whether we should seek a referendum. This was a controversial issue. There was pressure from the teachers' union. We all worked together and voted to go for the referendum. This, along with the superintendent search, has drawn the board together. We have focused in the right direction. We have worked together. We had our own opinions but we pulled together.

Board cohesiveness is based on shared values, and the act of identifying and asserting these shared values is a means of building cohesiveness.

4. Act on Values

The board shares certain values, using them as an explicit basis for its actions. Decisions are made both in the best interest of all children and with consideration of equal services for all children.

Despite the expected differences of opinion among board members, it is the quality of the decision-making process and the shared sense of basic values that can lead to decisions focused on the community and the needs of all its children. Interviewees describe such a process in a situation involving racial balance:

> Meetings were held at different schools. The key issue was whether the board could live with the consent order: what percent minority was allowable and how the individual schools would be balanced. There was pressure from the governor to vote for the consent order.

> What was good about the board's work with this issue was that the board actually sat down and discussed its educational ramifications. The board actually thought about the children and what was right for them.

Members draw other examples from a variety of situations. For example, during a student disciplinary hearing:

> The board had an opportunity to learn the background of the young man. This enabled the board to look at the situation differently. The board focused on what would be in the best interest of that young man. It demonstrated how the board thinks of individual children.

Finally, in some instances described, the values are more specifically focused on concrete goals:

> We started the process of computer labs in the schools. When they were first started, we had an aide as the person responsible. I felt we needed a certified teacher. I gave input to the superintendent, and the superintendent presented a proposal. The superintendent provided research on what was required. The board shared the value of increasing technology in the school district.

Board members typically talk about their understanding of shared values evolving from discussion about specific situations. Infrequently they reflect discussions that center on the question of what their shared values are, usually tied to a strategic planning process. Whether formal or informal in formulation, the explicit acknowledgment of shared values in determining board action contributes to effective group functioning.

5. Show Respect

Board members show respect by recognizing the value and importance of individual contributions. They trust each other's abilities, listen carefully, and honestly express viewpoints.

When these characteristics are present, board members are able to disagree without risking disapproval or damaging their ability to work together. Here's an example:

> When I first came on the board there was bad feeling among the board members. They didn't talk with each other. It didn't make for good board relations. Now the board gets along; its

members communicate; members can disagree without being disagreeable.

Here's another example that occurred in the context of discussion around a consent decree:

> The board members respect each other. There's no animosity. After a board meeting, we'll go out and have coffee together. We never let the sun go down on our wrath. In this case, although the board was split, it didn't carry over. We pulled back together.

A third example illustrates the importance of respect, this time in a workshop setting.

> The board went on a workshop with the administrators. We talked to each other as a board, conceptualizing issues related to education. We have respect for the opinions and attitudes of other board members. We recognize the problem and need for each person to have a comfort level. Board members listened to one another. We reached a conclusion that we could all live with.

Listening and considering an individual board member's point of view is critical to the development of respect. In one case an African American board member recalls arguing against transferring a staff person who was also African American:

> The board discussed transferring this individual and all approved the transfer except me. However, the decision was made with full respect for my point of view.

Afflicted with a lack of trust and respect, one board used a conflict resolution workshop as a way of overcoming its divisions. Says one of its members:

> The board had appointed a financial advisory committee. They came back with a report that the board ignored. The board members were ready to come to blows about the financial issues. The superintendent suggested we have a conflict resolution workshop, which we did. We met at a hotel over two weekends. It really helped. We get along better and better understand each other.

✓ What Boards Can Do

Board comments strongly support common understanding about school boards and about groups in general. If a board is to be effective, its members must work together to achieve common ends. To do this requires the understanding of and commitment to the process by which the board's work is achieved. Within this simple statement are the tensions of specific situations when interests and viewpoints are strongly held and substantially different. Without strong groundwork, these tensions may tear the best intentions of boards apart and substantially cripple their ability to achieve results.

Here are four action steps that may help boards to function effectively as groups:

1. *Commit to group functioning.* Board members should consciously and deliberately focus on the way they function and build common understanding and agreement on behavior expectations for the board. At the very least, members should commit to treating each board member with respect, honoring the right of each board member to hold and express a point of view on any topic under consideration, and sharing information as the basis for discussing issues.

2. *Provide board leadership.* Board members should consciously provide for strong board leadership, whether through a president or some form of shared leadership. Some board members must be recognized as acting for the board in developing, maintaining, and policing the behaviors required for effective group functioning.

3. *Develop and implement rules of operation.* Board members should reach explicit agreement on the process by which they will conduct their business. Each board should have a template of how issues are to be handled, independent of individual issues. This forms the standard of expected behavior and can guide thoughtful, deliberate consideration of decisions. The board should build in a review process that raises the level of self-consciousness with which the board functions.

4. *Discuss shared values.* Board members should draw from their discussions of district plans and their history of specific decisions to explore and articulate the values they share. They should consciously use these values as the underpinning of their decision making. These values link closely with the mission and goals of the district.

Exhibit 2.2 offers questions for you to consider in determining whether your board is effective.

EXHIBIT 2.2

Questions to Consider

Are there occasions when the board itself has acted in ways inconsistent with the district's deepest values?

Do board members say one thing in private and another thing in public?

Do you disagree openly with other members in board meetings?

At your board meetings, is there at least as much dialogue among members as there is between members and administrators?

Does the leadership of your board typically go out of its way to make sure that all members have the same information on important issues?

Has your board adopted some explicit goals for itself, distinct from goals it has for the total school district?

Are board members consistently able to hold confidential items in confidence?

Are there board meetings where discussions of the values of the district were key factors in reaching a conclusion on a problem?

Are board members able to speak their minds on key issues without fear that they will be ostracized by some members of your board?

Are values discussed explicitly at board meetings?

Once a decision is made, do all board members work together to see that it is accepted and carried out?

Are members of your board always respectful in their comments to other board members?

Chapter 3

Exercising Appropriate Authority

IN DISCUSSING THEIR ABILITY to act effectively, board members speak of the need to negotiate the delicate balance between exercising authority and supporting the school district's chief executive. Traditional governance wisdom suggests that you hire the best chief executive and then get out of his or her way. Board interviews indicate that it's not that simple. The superintendent's recommendation may be clearly contrary to the board's sense of what is important or supported by the community, or the superintendent may violate a prior understanding of proposed action. In these and other situations, boards feel they must exercise independent authority. In addition, the community often wants to see the board as independent of the superintendent. If the superintendent's recommendations are always approved, the board may be viewed as not sufficiently monitoring administrative actions.

In many of the interviews, members discuss their desire not to be labeled rubber stamps. As examples of effectiveness, board members cite times when they initiated actions, overruled the superintendent, or withstood the pressure of staff, community, and government:

> A proposed new grading policy was brought to the board. It would do away with letter grades and go to a pass-fail system with comments. The previous year they had approved a system with both letter grades and comments. I had said at that time I hoped they wouldn't do away with grades. The elementary school principal did not correct my misunderstanding. In the fall, when there were no grades on the first report card, everyone was confused and people were upset. There were two public workshops. The board and the public asked questions. Then the board voted in October whether to allow

the continuation of a no-grade report card on an experimental basis. It was discussed extensively and went to vote: 3-2 to continue the experiment until the end of the year and revisit it in May. I have been told that the recommendation of the teachers and administration in May will be to have letter grades with comment.

In this vignette and others identified by interviewees, four primary activities contribute to the ability of a board to effectively exercise its authority. Effective boards

Act with defined roles

Take initiative

Overrule the superintendent

Resist pressure

1. Act with Defined Roles

The board exercises authority, acting in a role predefined to make clear the relationship between the board and superintendent. Authority is defined and exercised through agenda setting, planning, and decision making, and by evaluating the superintendent.

Authority is often most effective when it is not exercised. The definition of the framework within which superintendent and staff have the authority to function without prior board review provides direction and efficiency to district management.

Many interviewees attributed effective board action to the defined roles played by board, board president, superintendent, and community. There are a number of variations. To some degree, the precise definition of roles depends on the style of each board and superintendent, and the relationship they have established, which is a function of the degree of collaboration or independence of the board and the amount of conflict in the roles. In many instances, board and superintendent are characterized as working smoothly together. In other instances, it appears that the superintendent is the issue, distracting from other problems.

One approach described by interviewees is that of staff and superintendent setting the stage for decision making by the board. In this instance, the staff obtained community input and gathered and analyzed data—all in preparation for the board's examination of alternatives:

We had a situation where there was a need to redraw the district lines because some schools had more students. The staff ran hearings. These were public meetings. We received lots of input from parents. Board members could go if they wanted to but they didn't have to. The staff looked carefully at the situation. They looked at the shortest routes to specific schools and the number of kids who fit and also worked with a data center as to the best way to shift children. The board then looked at different alternative plans. The board and administrative jobs were distinct.

Here is another, quite similar example, in this instance with an appointed board. Again, the superintendent is setting the stage for board review and decision making:

We went from a part-time to a full-time "techacademic" school program. The superintendent brought the idea to the board about five years ago. The board worked [at a board meeting] with a staff [group] of counselors, administrators, and teachers on where the school should be five years down the road. Then [the proposal] was tabled until the next meeting so the board could consider. The board asked questions and the superintendent provided more information. Then the board came to a decision to go ahead. We all had analyzed the situation and agreed.

Of course, a lot depends on the relationship between superintendent and board. Here's an example of a dysfunctional relationship:

We were given information about library books—$30,000 proposal for books and an information packet listing the books. But what does each library need and what about technology versus books? There was no plan presented. The board approved the library books 3-2 without a plan. Band uniforms—the need was justified but the plan wasn't there. What I'm suggesting in terms of plans and information represents a change in expectations, but there's a lack of administrative training to meet these expectations.

The flow of information and analysis from superintendent to board plays a significant role in the board's ability to exercise authority. Increased tension is the obvious outcome of a superintendent failing to supply information, even when requested. In cases such as these the board may make more than the usual effort to clearly exercise its control:

> In November, the director of curriculum retired. We were left with the position open. We could see that the responsibilities were too much for one person. We discussed breaking it into two positions. I persuaded other board members of the need for two positions. We came up with a plan for creating the new positions, one for elementary and one for secondary. We considered the people available and thought there were two who could do the job. One principal was not in the right place. He was in the process of changing. We sat down and went over the plan with them, meeting with staff and then going to the public.
>
> This showed the public and the school district that the board of education was taking control. The board looked at the background and experience of educators and looked at the direction it wanted for the school district. It needed to get the right people in the right positions. Before it felt that it was a rubber stamp board. If the superintendent said something, the board agreed.
>
> In this case, the board asked the superintendent for input and got no information. The board told the superintendent what they thought and didn't get feedback. The board worked as a total unit and reached consensus; the superintendent played a passive role.
>
> With this board, the five members speak up and listen to one another. They come to consensus on where we want to go.

Another dimension of these differentiated roles involves the community. In the first example of this section, the staff seeks public input in redrawing district lines. Here's another example concerning a hiring decision:

> The board is doing the final interviews in hiring administrators. We have a committee of parents, business representatives, staff, and the personnel director as the screening committee. They conduct interviews and forward names to the board. The board looks at the three names submitted, and the committee members meet with the board to give rationale. This gives community ownership. Parents can say they were a part of the process. It takes the burden off board members and the superintendent. It makes the process fair and unbiased.

The board members often characterize their roles as proactive while allowing administrative integrity. Here's an example concerning a reduction in the administration:

> When I was running for the board, one of the issues was that there were too many administrators. We downsized by one position this year. The administration is protective of its size and vocal in its support of the number of administrators. The administration has had to reconcile itself with the need to eliminate an administrator. The superintendent looked at reorganization and came up with a proactive plan. As a result, the administration is more efficient than before. We saved $47,000 in local money. This was a good example of the effectiveness of the board. The board sent signals and the superintendent responded. The board was effective in sending a message without forcing the administration—it wasn't slammed in the superintendent's face. The board then credited the administration, rather than saying it was about time. The superintendent made a presentation and the board accepted it.

In another case, the interviewee gives a more cynical view:

> The superintendent never worked against the vision, but it never would have gotten there without board leadership. We needed to give them credit, making it look like it was their idea. Another reflects a feeling—perhaps held by many—about the need for members to cultivate the capacity to act authoritatively:

> School boards become important when times are tough and resolution is necessary. You need to have a way of resolving difficulties.

2. Take Initiative

The board takes the lead in initiating actions that further its goals for the district.

Boards are typically cautious in taking initiative. But they talk about doing so when they feel the current course of action is not in the best interest of children or violates their understanding of what the district planned to do or what district policies would dictate.

There are numerous descriptions of board members taking such initiative. In one case involving an issue of new facilities, the board decides on a course of action distinct from the administrative suggestion. The interviewee states:

> The outcome was an effective one. The board was the final judge, exercising its authority to set major policy and representing what it felt the community thought to be in the best interest of children.

In several cases, board members characterize their actions as distinct from those of a rubber-stamp board. In one example, the interviewee discusses student discipline cases:

> In each case, the board talks about what's going to happen to this child versus the other students. It's a matter of balancing competing interests. There's a constant discussion and it is effective in maintaining school discipline. In the past the board was more of a rubber-stamp board. There is more discussion now.

Here's an example of board initiative within the curricular area, where boards are often less assertive:

> The board has made a conscious decision, expressed as a board goal, that the board should become more outspoken about its feelings regarding programs.

In another case, the board gets involved in a referendum after an earlier defeat:

> The board turns over the running of the schools to the superintendent and staff. We believed the first referendum went down because the administration didn't read where the new public was coming from. In the second, we got involved. We passed on our expertise—marketing, training, and development.

3. Overrule the Superintendent

The board makes decisions that are sometimes contrary to the recommendations of the superintendent.

In most of the cases cited, board members carefully consider the superintendent's recommendation but ultimately disagree and vote by a majority to take contrary action. Some members express the opinion that the ability of the board to exercise such authority ensures that the superintendent will make carefully researched and sensible recommendations.

In one situation there is a choice between building a new school or using trailers to provide additional building capacity:

> Four members of the board thought a new middle school was needed. The superintendent mobilized support against the new school but then honored the decision by the board to build a new school.

In another case, there is a need to set criteria for school choice:

> The superintendent laid out a set of criteria. I objected, stating that the criteria weren't in the spirit of the legislation. This was then hashed out for quite a while in a public meeting. We prevailed and the superintendent backed off. We changed the policy that he started out with.

In one instance, the interviewee believes the superintendent is recommending a personnel action based on information that's at least partially incorrect:

> The board has a mind of its own. We didn't just follow the administration. We didn't allow the administration to muscle us. The board showed that when you bring something to us, you better have your "ducks in a row." I made some calls to get additional information. If he was playing politics with the issues, I was willing to go outside the administration to get information.

And sometimes resolving a thorny issue means a powerful show of authority—overruling the superintendent:

> The board was in the middle of discussing raising graduation requirements and setting requirements for participation in extracurricular activities when I joined the board. A committee of administrators reviews policies and comes to the board for revisions. The board reviews [a first reading] and it goes back to the administration for revision. Then it comes to the board for a second reading and approval. In this case, there were four votes to change the policy, and they didn't waffle in the face of passionate administrative "pitch" not to make the policy changes. The administration said it would destroy kids if they got behind and couldn't participate in extracurricular activities. But the board got what it wanted. This was an example of

an effective board—speaking its mind in a proper employer-employee relationship with the superintendent, not just approving what the superintendent wanted.

4. Resist Pressure

The board makes decisions in the face of strong counterpressure from community, staff, the state, or others.

A number of interviewees speak of the board's action in resisting pressure, either from the community or the administration, in taking actions. Most often, it is a community group attempting to influence the board's decision. Some are student discipline decisions:

> There is an alternative school program. It's a new concept here, only in its second year. It's very overcrowded. Three students appealed to come back based on good behavior. Initially they were sent to the program based on a drug-related incident. There was no appeal policy. It was not dealt with in public session.
>
> We got past our emotions [and approved the appeal]. We did what was best for our district. We sent out the right message. Board members will make hard decisions; they are particularly difficult in the student personnel area as the odds of knowing a family involved is very high.

Sometimes it's a personnel decision, as in transferring an administrator from one school:

> There was a lot of heat from a group of people about the decision to transfer, but because it was a personnel decision, the board couldn't talk about it. But the board held together . . . because board members believe that doing the right thing is what counts.

In one instance, a board member opposes placing a new teacher in an overcrowded classroom and acted on this belief, despite the consequences:

> There was this situation of overcrowding in a kindergarten. The option was to put more students in the classroom or to hire a new teacher. The superintendent did not want to move the students to another school. She suggested placing an aide in the classroom. A certain group was vehemently opposed to this. They wanted an additional teacher. I observed, talked

with several teachers; people from the community came to the board to talk. I was empathetic with their situation and told them: "Don't give up." They misinterpreted my statement as an endorsement of their point of view. At the next meeting, I voted not to bring in a new kindergarten teacher. Some people were furious and withdrew business.

The board was effective in this situation, however. We weighed the whole situation and gave our decision. We emphasized that they should make the best of it. [Our guiding principle was] if you can't do it for all, you can't pick out one group for special treatment. The board members put their heads together, measured the situation, and took action.

In a few instances, the pressure comes from the superintendent. In the case of a new building:

A board member saw an issue and explained it to us; we took action; stuck to our guns, despite the superintendent's frustration over holding up the project.

✓ What Boards Can Do

Board members describe a proactive board role. To be effective, boards may define and assert a position on an issue that is contrary to the superintendent and community. A board may take action that is usually delegated to its superintendent. Board action will depend on the situation, the shared vision (superintendent-board) of what needs to be done, the willingness and skill of the superintendent to do what's required, and the mutual trust between board and superintendent. Boards have the authority but should exercise it judiciously. How can boards set the stage for a proper exercise of authority?

Here are three action steps to take:

1. *Define authority but use it sparingly.* Discuss with the superintendent and reach an understanding on the issues to come before the board, the information expected, the alternative proposals to be explored, the approach to board consultation, the administrative actions expected, and so forth. In the situations board members mentioned where they were exercising authority, they did so because they felt the superintendent and administration were not fully responsive. By planning in advance for the administrative support that is required, the use of authority can be minimized.

2. *Build a superintendent-board team concept.* Work with the superintendent in identifying the issues that are most important to the district and develop ways of addressing these issues. Authority then becomes jointly exercised with roles of administration and board defined in relation to specific issues.

3. *Emphasize mutual expectations and performance assessment.* Share with the superintendent your expectations for action; understand and commit to specific support actions the superintendent needs from the board; measure performance against these expectations.

It is a paradox that authority is most useful when it is not exercised. The board has the authority, but these actions build mutually supportive initiatives that make the exercise of authority less relevant. When the mutual action breaks down, authority must be used—a step to be avoided if possible.

Exhibit 3.1 offers questions to consider when assessing your board's use of its authority.

EXHIBIT 3.1

Questions to Consider

Do your board and superintendent usually advocate the same actions?

Does your board sharply question certain administrative proposals, requiring the superintendent to reconsider the recommendation?

Is your board always involved in decisions that are important to the future of education in your district?

Will your board often persuade the superintendent to change his or her mind about recommendations?

Does your board often request additional information before making a decision?

Does your board often discuss its role in district management?

Does your board usually accept recommendations from the administration with little questioning?

Do the board president and superintendent confer so that differences of opinion are identified?

Is yours a rubber-stamp board?

Does your board often act independently of the superintendent's recommendations?

Is your board outspoken in its views about programs?

Will your board reverse its position based on pressure from the community?

Chapter 4

Connecting to the Community

THE BOARD SERVES as a liaison between the district and the community. An effective board understands what the community wants and explains to the community what it believes to be in the best interest of children.

The process works both ways. The long-established tradition of local control of education is based on the value of the community shaping its schools and of the schools "belonging" to the community. This close relationship contributes to greater community participation in the education of its children and interest in how the schools operate. Even in the context of current times, which see a decline in the number of households with school-age children, fewer volunteers, and a diminishing respect for public schools, interest in education is intense.

As communities become more diverse, so do their values. Building understanding and support becomes an increasing challenge. The board's role in explaining actions to the community and ensuring consideration of all points of view becomes increasingly important.

The board's relationship with the community is multifaceted and includes a variety of mechanisms, both formal and informal, for presenting information to the public and soliciting community input. These run the gamut from meetings and public hearings to casual conversations in the supermarket aisle or a constituent's living room. The quality of the board-community relationship faces one of its most severe tests when the possibility of increased taxes is on the horizon.

> We passed a referendum for capital improvements in 1994. The current buildings were built in the 1930s. We had tried for twenty-one years to get a referendum passed. The school buildings were in bad shape. One option was to build a new school. We bought property years ago, anticipating building. The board surveyed the

community and there was a feeling that we should renovate. We tried to spearhead the opportunities for people to understand. The board members were out every night in advance of the referendum. Everyone worked together. There was a common purpose and goal. We were feeling a part of the community.

What was effective about this board effort was that we were a liaison between the community and the educational system. We understood community preferences. Then we translated these into an action plan and came back to the community. We were able to persuade others of the need. This represented the vision of the board, seeing the need and the benefits. All of the board members had either children or grandchildren in the district. We had a common vision on this issue. The superintendent was instrumental in pulling everything together. It was a joint board-superintendent perspective in seeing the need. A committee was formed by the board, for strategic planning; the buildings became a focus.

In interviews board members cited five primary activities as contributing to the kind of relationship with the community that contributes to board effectiveness. Boards relate well to the public when they

Structure community involvement

Obtain input

Explain actions

Facilitate information flow

Connect with the internal community

1. Structure Community Involvement

The board defines and structures the involvement of constituents in the governance process.

Much of this structured involvement is ongoing and systematic, such as in strategic planning. In this example the board had difficulty accepting the committee report, but the interviewee still sees it as illustrating effective board leadership:

We developed a strategic plan for the district. The state mandated that we do so. We decided we would do it right. We brought in a facilitator from outside the district. We set up a strategic planning committee of twenty-one persons. The committee was made up of people across the board, including some board members. The committee plan came back to the full board but wasn't viewed as positively by board members who weren't part of the process. However, it did show good leadership and a clear outline of our role.

Here's another example of a similar process:

> We set up strategic planning committees. We brought together committees of students, teachers, and parents to deal with curriculum and finance issues. One of the board members suggested it. It got everyone involved and got plans for individual schools.

In addition to structured long-term processes, board members say they improve their effectiveness by establishing structures for community involvement on individual, short-term issues and in situations that create intense community pressure. One example had to do with a proposed wellness center.

> The state offered us dollars to provide a wellness center in the schools. One board member was adamantly opposed and very vocal. One board member was supportive. There were a lot of hearings. There was an extremely vocal group adamantly opposed. There were moral issues and tax issues. Board members attended hearings. For example, there was one sponsored by the Christian Coalition; board members and administration came. The board did a good job of investigation, polling the community.

Another interviewee speaks about the effectiveness of the board in the much less volatile planning for a new elementary school.

> We developed community committees—a site selection committee, a building design committee. We involved the community from the beginning. This was somewhat unique. The community bought in; there were changes made based on community input. We got outside. It wasn't just an education perspective—we included business, parents, and teachers. We gave people ownership of the project. It was effective.

This example illustrates a technique that has proven successful in many districts—using community committees for specific purposes. By choosing citizens representing a variety of viewpoints as committee members, it is possible to fashion proposals with broader support and to communicate the importance placed on broad input.

2. Obtain Input

The board listens to community groups, obtaining public input on important matters and listening to constituents' concerns. Before reaching final decisions, the board requests input from those affected and keeps informed of the impact of its actions on the community.

Depending on the volatility of the issue, soliciting input can be a painful process. That is true in this example; a final resolution of the issue may be years down the road:

> The court order assigned high school students to particular schools. It wasn't equitable. Meetings were tearing the district apart. Meetings went on for hours. People were screaming at each other. The idea of choice emerged from this. [The board president had knowledge of policy alternatives so could generate this idea.] The first year it lost by one vote. We fought with the state board about putting programs in the schools. Finally, in 1992, we gave all ninth grades their choice. We had to go to the judge. The judge denied the order [for certain students]. The first year of open enrollment was 1994–95.
>
> The board educated each other. We listened to the community. We got the pulse of what the community wanted. In the end, all seven of us thought it was a good idea. The board was clearly in it for the long run. The board needs to have a vision and be patient.

Sometimes, members say, boards need to reach out in less-structured ways to gauge the community pulse, sometimes meeting in constituents' homes. This case involved the referendum:

> After three or four failed attempts, we went to the people through small meetings in peoples' living rooms. The five board members were born and raised in the district. They were all well known and knew whom to call to have people gather at their home.

Sometimes a not-so-restful retreat is held:

I'm in favor of operating in an open way. I think we should have a retreat, open to the public, to brainstorm around what the school district should be doing. Then administration and board can put the problems and solutions together. This is a lot better than the superintendent telephoning individual school board members to get recommendations. It presents a picture to the public of an open approach.

The biggest mistake we have made in the past was not dealing with the public as they really exist. If you keep information from the public or don't deal with issues head on, it creates problems. For example, it took us eight years to acknowledge the racial balance issue. Now we don't let things get too far before we deal with them. Board members respect each other. We don't stop talking until the issue is resolved.

Several interviewees used examples to characterize a general approach of the board. One example was in the context of considering a new ROTC program:

There was ample opportunity for public discussion. The board sets the rules with an hour and a half for discussion, then general business. This illustrated board effectiveness in that everyone was open-minded and asked a lot of questions. The decision was made based on information, not based on a strong, emotional public.

Another example involved a decision to include a nonvoting student member of the school board.

We were able to have an open, honest discussion about this issue in public. We were able to have an open discussion with the audience and student reps. They were able to be open and honest and to listen to what we were hearing rather than making a decision based on preconceived values.

One board member talks about the consequences and backtracking that can result when boards don't solicit community input:

We had a recommendation from the superintendent to close a department at one school because there weren't enough kids. The board took the recommendation with the proviso that the kids in the program could transfer. At the next meeting, the kids and parents came to the board meeting to plead to keep the program open. We decided to keep the program open. We should have talked with the kids and parents before making the initial recommendation. We had the same situation with another program and we kept it, trying to get more kids involved.

3. Explain Actions

The board goes to the community to explain proposed and current board positions and actions, as well as district programs. The board communicates the results of decisions to those affected.

Often board members view themselves as effective when they are proactive in taking their priorities to the community to gain understanding and support. In this case their actions relate to their push for passage of a funding referendum:

> We have a capital referendum coming up this year. The priority last fall was to improve community relations to assure the passage of the referendum. There's a vocal negative group. Two board members had a meeting with this group. Their primary concern was that "no one listens to us." I gave them my home telephone number. It has been an extremely positive step forward. And the referendum was passed. The members of the community said that the board must sell it. The board took the initiative and created a community task force led by a retired corporate executive. There were two public meetings; five people came to the first and nine to the second. So we took the show on the road—to the Lions' Club and the Rotary Club. The board must get the community involved. It only passed by eighty-four votes. The board did a soft sell, working behind the scenes.

Explaining and defending actions on controversial decisions often calls for considerable courage. To be effective, says one board member, you have to stand your ground; be ready for criticism; be aware of pressures; don't let family suffer; be positive, upbeat, and on guard.

4. Facilitate Information Flow

The board provides for an open flow of relevant information to and from the community.

Board members include in their examples of effective board action the way in which they promote the flow of information and understanding between community and board. One member talks about the effectiveness of public workshops held by the board to discuss a controversial new grading policy:

> This was effective in that we debated the issue and got the issue out to the public. The board did not rubber stamp the administration recommendation. There was a full debate. We thoroughly considered the recommendation; we made the administration think about their recommendation. We got more information on the issue of grades and made the administration do its job. We made them justify the need for change, that is, how it would benefit children. Agree or disagree, the superintendent knew, and through workshops the public knew, why this was going on. The frustration is that sometimes citizens aren't informed.

One board member talks about the danger of cutting off communication and the positive, and perhaps unanticipated, effects when boards are receptive to the free exchange of information:

> On the kindergarten overcrowding: at a board meeting, a group wanted to express their views. The president decided to cut off discussion. He sent a negative message to the group that the board members were not good listeners. He could have suggested that they get on the agenda of the next meeting. Now we allow an open mike situation to allow the community to express its opinion. It's a good improvement. We're getting more influential members of the community at board meetings and board members invited to other groups.

In many instances, certain segments of the community pressure board members to make a decision or renege on a previous action. An effective board can choose to respond to legitimate community concerns or stand firm in the face of pressure to take actions not in the best interest of the schools. The following pressure-filled situation proves particularly difficult because the full information couldn't be disclosed to protect the staff member involved:

> We let a minority teacher go. The minority community came down hard on me and on the board as a whole for making such a decision. However, the teacher didn't give evidence that she had done what was required. So the board let her go. I caught

much of the negative comment from the community. There was picketing at the board meeting. But the board can't disclose personnel information so it was difficult to defend our decision. The board stood its ground.

5. Connect with the Internal Community

Although distinct from the usual definition of *community*, teachers and other staff form a critically important constituent group, and the discussion of board action—structuring involvement, obtaining input, explaining actions, and facilitating information flow—has an appropriate interpretation, even though it must be redefined by their status as employees.

In other words, the external community empowers the board through the election process; the teachers and staff bring the authority of professional expertise as collaborative members of the team seeking educational improvement.

In their interviews, school board members cite many examples of their relationship with staff as contributing to board effectiveness, particularly emphasizing the way in which that relationship is structured and the importance of open communication. One example has to do with "win-win" negotiations:

> Two years ago we tried a new approach to negotiations with the teachers. The teachers had felt that the traditional contract negotiations were demeaning and the board wasn't involved in the past. So a "win-win" approach to negotiations was suggested. The board and teachers went through training. In the end, the win-win approach didn't work because the financial package didn't work. The teachers lacked trust in the board and thought the board was hiding money.

> There was a board committee of four persons involved. The teachers had the impression that the four board members could make decisions since they constituted a quorum of the board. Four board members were chosen—two new ones, interested in finance and supportive of teachers, and two others who were "pro-stability." The two who had been pro-teacher became negative.

> The board worked together on this. The financial part was difficult. Board members had to build an understanding of finances and their own budget. No one was grandstanding.

Ultimately, the effectiveness was due to people doing their homework, spending time with each other to be sure that issues were discussed and all understood.

It was the opportunity the board created to spend time with teachers and to be sure issues were discussed and understood that led to this interviewee considering these actions as contributing to board effectiveness.

In another example, a board member talks about a different structure:

> We have worked with the local education association on shared decision making. One issue that concerned them was inclusion. A group of teachers approached the board. Teachers were feeling bad because they had not had a good relationship with the board. Now the local education association meets with the board for thirty minutes before the regular board meeting.

In a third example, the interviewee discusses a monthly board breakfast with representatives of staff:

> This example involved contract negotiations. We work through our superintendent. We don't have outside professionals. We have been successful in doing this quickly and without high expense to the taxpayers. The teachers have accepted what we have done. The tone of the discussion has been collegial. We have close contact with the staff. We meet with the staff frequently. They feel free to discuss their concerns with board members. We have a board breakfast with staff once a month. It maintains a level of dialogue and trust.

Interviewees cite other examples where the board acts systematically to structure involvement, but in the context of a specific issue. One example is in the area of negotiations where an interviewee discusses a board interest in pay for performance and the approach of a joint union-system committee to study the issue:

> One of the issues addressed by the board was pay for performance. It lost by two votes. We made a mistake. We walked into negotiations with teachers, saying we would do it. Both sides dug in their heels. We set up a committee to examine the issue: ten system persons and ten union persons. We had 170 hours of meetings. The trust between the administrators and the teachers was destroyed at the bargaining table. The committee primarily rebuilt trust. The committee put forward a proposal that lost by three votes in a full union vote. The board

person, in negotiation strategy, made a mistake. He met in executive session with the board to recast strategy. The union guy didn't endorse and the mistake cost the vote.

Another case, related to the riffing (reduction in number of teachers) and tenure of teachers, emphasizes listening to all sides of an issue:

> The board has opted to give teachers a hearing before they are riffed to be sure the information they have about the teacher's situation is correct and to have insight into the situation of the individual affected. The superintendent recommended there be no hearing, but the board reached consensus that there should be a hearing. There was an uproar about the existing policy, complaints from staff and parents, and the board felt it should respond. In some instances, the board overturned the superintendent's recommendation based upon further investigation.
>
> This board response demonstrates effectiveness because the board was sending a message to staff, community, and parents that the board is willing to be fair and open-minded. The board has taken steps to hear all sides of an issue and to make sure it is making the best decision. Over the past six years, the board has evolved from a rubber-stamp board to a diverse, educated, open board. Each board member feels strongly about being open.

Although the topics and focus differ, the principles for an effective board-teacher relationship are strikingly similar to the standards for a healthy board-community connection. Structure, two-way communication, and quality of information are key, and they reflect the nature of shared decision making and of negotiations based on mutual trust.

✓ What Boards Can Do

At the core, school boards form a bridge between the community and the school system or district serving that community. The quality and effectiveness of that bridge depends on the board's relationship with its community. Effective boards must center efforts on building trust—the quality of community understanding and support of board and district actions.

Here are three actions that boards can take:

1. *Provide structured community participation for both short- and longer-term issues.* Through strategic and long-term planning processes, board meetings with specific opportunities for community input, advisory task forces, surveys, focus groups, and many other structures, the board can

provide opportunities for community input and participation. This participation should be well defined and understood, viewed as adequate by the community, and consistently administered so the public can rely on it as a legitimate way of participating in board decisions.

2. *Maintain the two-way communication implicit in an effective relationship.* Boards are conscious of obtaining community input but often forget the importance of explaining the policy alternatives and their rationale to the community so the community may understand the reasons for board decisions. The board must structure modes of communication through issue papers, newsletters, Internet, press releases, briefing sessions, and so on, that ensure community understanding of board action.

3. *Use information for effective action.* Boards should recognize the benefit of investing time, money, and staff in providing information that is well formulated and conveyed. Busy citizens must understand complex issues and recognize the way boards have used their input.

Exhibit 4.1 provides questions to consider when determining how effectively your board is connecting to the community.

EXHIBIT 4.1
Questions to Consider

Does your board have formal structures and procedures for involving the community?

Is a written report including the board's activities periodically prepared and distributed publicly?

Does your board communicate its decisions to all who are affected by them?

If your board thinks that an important group of constituents is likely to disagree with an action you are considering, will you make sure you learn how they feel before you make the decision?

Does your board and its members maintain channels of communication with key community leaders?

Has your board formed ad hoc committees or task forces that include staff and community representatives as well as board members?

Is your board as attentive to how it reaches conclusions as it is to what is decided?

Are there board meetings where you give explicit attention to the concerns of the community?

Does the board periodically obtain information on the perspectives of staff and community?

Before reaching a decision on important issues, does your board usually request input from persons likely to be affected by the decision?

Is your board always aware of the impact its decisions will have within your service community?

Does the administration often report to the board on the concerns of those the school district serves?

Chapter 5

Working Toward Board Improvement

WHEN BOARDS TALK about effectiveness, one area they center on is self-improvement. This shouldn't be surprising. Forty percent of board members have three or fewer years of experience. They say in interviews that it takes them two years to understand their board roles well enough to be fully effective. Furthermore, it is through ad hoc, unplanned contact with other board members and the superintendent that they learn much of what they know.[1]

In their quest for self-improvement, boards seek outside assistance and cultivate leadership and membership. Board members describe actions that include reflection on and adjustment of their responsibilities and authority. Interviewees discuss activities that assist new members in understanding their responsibilities:

> We had an issue of new board members and how to draw them in to the way we were working. A conflict resolution workshop was suggested. We met on two weekends and had an outside consultant. The workshop brought out a lot. The consultant was able to assert control of what went on. She made the board members be honest in what was discussed and feel comfortable in doing so. By working with the board in this way, she was able to help the board members all come together in their thinking.

A few board members, in discussing their examples of board effectiveness, speak strongly of the contribution of *three* self-improvement activities in contributing to this effectiveness. They see how critical it is for boards to

Cultivate leadership

Assess competence

Obtain assistance

1. Cultivate Leadership

The board actively seeks board members to run for office or to fill positions when resignations occur during a term.

Board members speak of examples of effectiveness connected to recruiting effective board members. With elected boards, this is accomplished through seeking out qualified individuals to fill unexpired terms and persuading them to serve.

> The board has the capacity to handle this kind of situation because the board has camaraderie. Board members are willing to stay the extra time. It's the openness of the board. The board members can argue and disagree, but still talk to each other. If something is on our minds we try to get it out. When I was first considered for filling the unexpired term of the board member leaving, the other board members looked for that characteristic in interviewing me. I knew the majority of the board members real well; I went to school with some of them.

Here's another example, this time involving a superintendent search:

> The board has worked well in working through this. The board is honest and open with each other. We looked at the issues—what's best for kids. There were no cliques, no hidden agendas. This facilitated doing a good job. We were honest and straightforward in getting input from others. We were discreet; there were no leaks. The board has this capacity because we are all honest and want to do a good job. Six of eight members are college graduates. Five have advanced degrees. The superintendent and the board value the recruitment of levelheaded, sensible persons to run for the board.

2. Assess Competence

Board members reflect, gain perspective, and think about what it means to hold office. The board seeks and considers information and feedback on its performance. The board diagnoses its strengths and limitations and examines its mistakes.

Only about 25 percent of school boards regularly participate in self-evaluation. Yet interviewees and experts concur that there must be the opportunity for boards to assess their competence.[2]

Board interviewees often talk about the importance of self-evaluation as a future plan. One member gives a response, echoed by many: "The board is looking at models for self-evaluation, but hasn't done it yet." Another makes the point: "There has not been a board self-evaluation, although that is an interesting idea." Some interviewees did reflect current evaluation activities:

> We had two board workshops this year. The board evaluates its own operation. We need a board-effectiveness tool that is specific for our district. In the past we worked with a general questionnaire. Whatever is done can't be last-minute.

Although other sections of our interviews led to board member descriptions of self-evaluation activities, there is one instance of such activity connected directly to a vignette illustrating board effectiveness. In this instance, the assessment is precipitated by the board members' belief that a colleague is using his position unwisely:

> Two school board members believe one other member is using his position to gain advantage for his child in school. Teachers think that individual school board members have more power than they have. The two school board members talked with the superintendent about a positive ethics policy to deal with the school district. You can have a similar issue when a teacher has the student of an administrator. Businessmen on the board have conducted business with the school. We need specific rules and guidelines. Looking to the future, this helps us define our effectiveness. We need to be effective in self-policing. By passing such a policy, we can address distrust and educate administration and staff that school board members have no greater privilege than other members of the community.

3. Obtain Assistance

The board seeks and uses the assistance of outside consultants or facilitators in accomplishing its work. The board assists new and old members in functioning as part of the whole.

School board members are relatively inexperienced. They lack systematic, comprehensive training for their complex work. Many interviewees, in emphasizing the importance of their development as board members, cite the value of using outside assistance. Usually a particular situation triggers the use of outside help. Most of these instances involve strategic planning; others center on negotiations, conflict resolution, and desegregation. But in all cases, the benefit is broader, influencing overall board effectiveness.

In this example, the board organizes two retreats a year and uses this time to set goals for itself and expectations for the superintendent:

> Members have made a conscious decision, expressed as a board goal, that the board should become more outspoken on its feelings regarding programs, like the reading program. The board should let its constituents know the actions and progress directly from the board.
>
> This has been helped by a program of two board retreats a year, which was started two years ago. The board decided to get away and talk about things without making decisions. We start Friday afternoon, spend the night, and continue all day Saturday. The superintendent is there. Part of a retreat involved the superintendent's evaluation. This was helpful in setting expectations. The student board member came too.

In another, a consultant helps new and old members learn to function as a group:

> We had an issue of new board members and how to draw them in to the way we were working. A conflict resolution workshop was suggested. We met on two weekends and had an outside consultant. The workshop brought out a lot. The consultant was able to assert control of what went on. She made the board members be honest in what was discussed and to feel comfortable in doing so. By working with the board in this way, she was able to help the board all come together in their thinking.

In a third case, the board plans a referendum and uses consultants in developing and updating its long-range plan.

> We sought and received voter approval on a referendum in 1993. We followed a planning process where the superintendent and board worked together. We asked for $85 million. We have a long-range plan, updated annually, which we project three to five years into the future. We involve parents, citizens, as well as the superintendent and board. We bring in a consultant from time to time—five to six times in eleven years. We conducted a feasibility study, pricing the changes needed,

looking at compliance issues, general upkeep, and so on. We conducted a detailed analysis to be sure there was no feeling of inequitable treatment.

This illustrates board effectiveness—first because the referendum was passed and also because of the process. We generated lots of information which was shared as much as possible. There was lots of involvement. It was an open process. We went to parent groups and civic associations and service clubs, promoting understanding.

In a fourth example, the board member represents an appointed vocational board, and the conference cited is a joint venture of the board and administration.

The board went on a workshop with the administrators. We talked to each other as a board, conceptualizing issues related to education. We have respect for the opinions and attitudes of other board members. We recognize the problem and need for each person to have a comfort level. Board members listened to one another. We reached a conclusion that we could all live with. The board tends to be single-minded. We don't strongly differ. Some people are more influential than others. We went through a workshop on brain dominance and the board is balanced. Since board members are appointed, we don't have a constituency issue.

Although the examples represent assistance in the strategic planning aspect of the board's work, other examples of outside assistance were in response to crisis situations. One example concerns solving problems of racial balance:

We identified a consultant who came, free of charge, to meet with us. We had two, three days of meetings. We listed what we wanted out of the decision and brainstormed options on feeder patterns and balance. The board reached consensus.

Of course, not all board members agree on the value of consultants:

There's a need for board members to have rudimentary facts about the relationship between the administration and the board—how school board members work with each other and what they are entitled to expect from the superintendent. Consultants tell school board members how they should behave, but they come with a bias. School board members shouldn't be involved in personnel, but school boards can't wait for the superintendent in all situations. School board members need to find their own conclusion. They need to be exposed to a variety of perspectives about how the school board should conduct itself.

However, some see the need—in retrospect:

Selecting a superintendent was a disaster. The minorities wanted a minority, so there was a bias toward selecting minorities. We needed consultants or other means to find talent. We didn't probe deeply enough.

✓ What Boards Can Do

Recognition of the need for board reflection and action toward self-improvement is elusive; it is strongly recognized by experts and some board members but ignored by others. Boards must build understanding and support for these activities.

Three actions are suggested:

1. *Cultivate advocates and champions.* Those who favor the reflective, evaluative approach to self-improvement typically have experience with the processes involved. Encourage the superintendent, community leaders, and others to advocate and support such activities.

2. *Link development with important issues.* Reflect on board operation and values as they relate to specific issues of importance to the community. The examples in this chapter are linked with desegregation, negotiations, strategic planning, and other important issues. When the stakes are high and the outcome visible, attention focuses on how well the board is doing its work.

3. *Build active community participants.* Structure community involvement to encourage the participation of the most effective community leaders. Cultivate their interest as potential school board members. The conscious recruitment of broad community leadership will encourage effective board leadership in the future.

Exhibit 5.1 provides questions to consider when you are evaluating a board's self-improvement efforts.

EXHIBIT 5.1

Questions to Consider

Do members participate in board discussions about what you should do differently as a result of a mistake the board made?

At least once every two years, does your board have a retreat or special session to examine your performance—to ask how well you are doing as a board?

Does your board periodically set aside time to learn more about important issues facing school districts like the one you govern?

Does your board explicitly cultivate future leaders for the board or rely on the natural emergence of leaders?

Do board members typically rely on observation and informal discussions to learn about their roles and responsibilities?

When a new member joins the board, do you make sure that someone serves as a mentor to help this person learn the ropes?

Do you have board discussions about the effectiveness of your performance?

Have you participated in discussions with new members about the roles and responsibilities of a board member?

Does your board seek outside assistance in considering its work?

Have you ever received feedback on your performance as a member of your board?

Does your board allocate organizational funds for the purpose of board education and development?

Has your board conducted an explicit examination of its roles and responsibilities?

Chapter 6

Acting Strategically

BOARD MEMBERS discuss and resolve issues that are central to helping children learn. They plan systematically and for the long term, taking into consideration the needs and concerns of internal and external constituents, all the while balancing reality and politics. They match plans against results. They organize responsibilities and authority between superintendent and board to adjust for strengths and weaknesses. Boards that can accomplish these tasks can deal effectively with crises, especially when they have no choice but to act.

We had a problem with racial balance. There were public hearings. The differences were deep-rooted. We were trying to figure out what to do.

Here's how it happened. We tried first meeting with a larger group and then with the board. The board was able to get together. The top administration and the board were involved. The administration often does what it thinks the board wants. The superintendent will be very cautious without board support, and that interferes with innovation. Everyone was frustrated. We threw ideas out on the table. We involved people from all sides to plan, including the superintendent.

We had two to three days of meetings; a large corporation volunteered its human resources expert to assist. We listed what we wanted out of the decision and brainstormed options. The board reached consensus.

We then moved out to the public. With board consensus, the public didn't know how to deal with us. A state board member acted as an ally. We stayed on higher ground than our opponents.

This was a good example of board effectiveness. We dealt with the problem despite difficulty and in the face of criticism. We were willing to step forward and take the heat. We dealt with things in public; we didn't talk behind closed doors. We knew you can't deal privately with this kind of issue and get anywhere. We built trust with the community. Why was the board able to do this? We had to. It was an intense subject, larger than the board. We had to act; we couldn't ignore it.

Interviewees identified five primary activities that contribute to effective, strategic action on the part of school boards. They emphasize the need for boards to

Address critical issues

Plan

Organize

Consider context

Evaluate

1. Address Critical Issues

The board confronts rather than avoids the issues that shape the school district and its program. These issues may be closely linked with programs, with broad concepts, or with policy. They may relate to the superintendent's leadership.

Deciding what's critical is the hardest part. It's not always clear and boards have difficulty deciding. For boards, critical issues are determined by three criteria:

1. They are the issues of greatest importance to the district; they will have an impact on student learning.

2. They are issues in dire need of resolution; the controversy around them interferes with accomplishing educational purposes.

3. They are issues in which the board's participation is really important because of the board's authority to govern, its independence from the superintendent, and its role in representing the community.

Several examples illustrate this activity. In some the board considers changes in its responsibility for making educational decisions:

In the past, the board has not felt it had the authority to make decisions on instructional matters. It is currently evaluating itself and feeling it is responsible for educational decisions. Next meeting, we will adopt a policy on reading. Our discussion of these matters has been open and honest. We receive input from the professional but are making board decisions.

This board is rethinking the importance of its role in instructional decisions. In the past, members have relied on the superintendent's recommendation, showing caution about delving into areas such as curriculum, where professional competence is so important. Here the board is asserting additional authority because of the critical nature of instructional decisions:

I define board effectiveness as directly related to the board's role as a policymaking body. The issue of the desegregation appeal was just such a policy initiative expressing the district's philosophy regarding diversity.

Another board member cites a decision on the middle school concept as illustrating board effectiveness because the issue was important and because the decision was made with some independence from the superintendent's viewpoint:

The board decided on the middle school concept. It's new. We discussed it. We all understood the issue. We had background information. We reached agreement.

The board is open-minded for the most part. You have to get their attention. They are not afraid to make a decision even if it is contrary to the superintendent.

2. Plan

The board plans longer-term and systematically for results. The board reviews strategies for achieving long-term goals. It discusses where the organization should be headed into the future.

Boards tend to plan less than they should. The problem is that planning is hard work; results aren't immediately evident, and boards focus on the more immediate problems presented by the superintendent and community in day-to-day district operations.

Members cite several examples of effective board action where planning is important. Most cases describe clear, multifaceted processes, some for broad strategic purposes and others to address specific critical situations. Here is an example using a planning committee of board members and community and staff representatives:

> We developed a strategic plan for the district. We set up a strategic planning committee of twenty-one persons. The committee plan came back to the full board. It showed good leadership and a clear outline of our role.

In one example, the interviewee makes explicit both the rational and political aspects of strategic planning:

> Getting the proposals approved required rational planning and strategizing. We had to understand both the substantive clarity and the political strategy. School boards become important when times are tough and resolution is necessary. You need to have a way of resolving difficulties.

In some instances, the references to planning involve specific situations. In one confrontation with a minority group, the board discusses various strategies and decides to postpone action:

> So we let it go. Then we got a new superintendent. He addressed the problem with a new strategic plan. This demonstrated our effectiveness because we listened to the community and were able to step back, look at the situation, and start over again.

3. Organize

The board considers and adjusts the roles of board, superintendent, and individual board members in meeting new situations and in accomplishing the work of the district.

Organizing is a continuous process of testing and modifying the board's role to fit particular situations. Here's a case where a board member acts directly with a principal, questioning an administrative action, and the board raises the question of whether the member's behavior was appropriate:

> The superintendent is the CEO. We regard board behavior as important to monitor and confront where it intrudes on the

ability of the superintendent to do his job. For example, we have a high school where the suspension rate is lower than in other schools. A board member called the principal and told him that he needs to suspend kids more frequently. We confronted this in a board meeting. Why did you do that? We tried to get board members to focus on the policy of how an issue like this should be handled.

In several cases, the board responds to specific situations by playing a more action-oriented role than usual. In one example, concerning a referendum, the board member states:

> We believe the first referendum went down because the administration didn't read where the new public was coming from. In the second we got involved. We passed on our expertise—marketing, training, and development.

In another example a board member plays an active role to supplement superintendent leadership:

> I knew we had to work better together but we couldn't compromise on the clear path. These were people of good faith. The superintendent and I did some planning as to how we could shape proposals to the board. The superintendent never worked against the vision, but it never would have gotten there without board leadership. We never had a superintendent who was a real leader.

There are several examples of individual board members defining more proactive roles as monitors of district action regarding individual students. In one case, a board member describes assisting in several situations:

> Kids were playing no-touch football. One kid (A) got rough and knocked the second kid (B) down. B took a swing at A. B was suspended. I called and wanted to find out what really happened. Then the suspension was dropped.
>
> In another case, a fifteen-year-old girl got pregnant. When she was trying to get ahead and trying to come to the vo-tech school, she brought her infant. She got the run-around. She couldn't have lunch; couldn't put her child in day care. I'm investigating now. Most people on the outside don't know how to deal with red tape. I'm helping people cut through red tape in cases that are unfair.

In another situation, a board member investigates a contract bid and saves the board money. As a consequence, the board views him as having special expertise: "Now the board defers to my judgment, as in choosing an architect for another school. Such deference is a little frightening."

4. Consider Context

The board considers the needs and concerns of internal and external constituents. When discussing issues, the board takes into account community needs and opinion, as well as national education policy and recommendations. The board makes decisions with this larger perspective in mind.

The consideration of context is mentioned as an important strategic action in school board effectiveness in several vignettes. Since the context includes the community, many of these examples also illustrate the way the boards relate to the public, as described in Chapter Four. As used here, these examples link the community relationship to the appropriateness of specific decisions. Sometimes this relationship involves specific input; other times it illustrates the importance of the board understanding community needs and appreciating the importance of community support in making decisions.

One interviewee illustrates accommodating to community views by modifying the approach to solving a problem:

> We made a decision not to have a wellness center in the district. We have the lowest per-capita income in the state and I was in favor of it; I thought we needed it. But the majority won. There was concern about sex education and advice. There was a big push against the wellness center from the religious community. So we went back to the people who opposed the center and asked them for help. They truly believed in their position. Now we have formed a committee of parents and teachers to provide a wellness center.
>
> You have to understand where people are coming from. You need to understand that people are distrustful of big government. They are fearful of the ultimate power of the dollars. You have to convince people; and if you can't, you have to find an alternative solution. That's what we did.

Another says:

We let the professionals do the job but what they propose may not always be the best way. The satisfaction in the decision was that it was a community decision. I ran for the school board in the first place to be sure the schools reflected the community's idea of education.

Another board member discusses the financial responsibility of the board's decisions:

Here the board is reflecting the community and charged to be aware of this. We must understand and act responsibly. We're spending the community's money.

In one vignette, a board member is discussing a decision in which the superintendent's initial viewpoint was different from that of the board. This case illustrates how the board used the community context to give perspective to a decision:

In this situation, the board was determining what courses should be taught. For example, the community needs welders, but kids don't want to be welders. What happens when a program loses interest but there's a lot of need for it? We were effective in letting the administration know that we didn't want to eliminate programs that were needed where ninth graders don't see the need. If the board hadn't acted, the superintendent might have acted differently. It provided perspective of community needs. We got the business community involved in helping.

5. Evaluate

The board matches plans against results. It assesses the superintendent, matching expectations against performance. It explores issues in the broader context of the effectiveness of board operations.

The board members cite evaluation in many of their vignettes as central actions leading to board effectiveness. The evaluation is of several types, including, as would be expected, the evaluation of the superintendent:

The superintendent evaluation process was put in the superintendent's contract. This spring, the board had three sessions to collect and collate information and provide the superintendent with feedback. It was a merit-based process.

This process, because it was personnel, gave the board the opportunity to discuss in private.

In this next case, the board was attempting to implement a systematic evaluation program but the superintendent was less than fully responsive. It illustrates the difficulty of implementing evaluation programs and the importance of the superintendent's cooperation in doing so.

> A motion was introduced and passed by a 3-2 vote to have the administration conduct a self-evaluation regarding the programs, teaching, and administration. The administration was given six months to conduct the evaluation. But the superintendent didn't do what he was asked to do. The board has not taken any action even when it was brought up. This suggests ineffectiveness by the board. The board doesn't evaluate the superintendent.

✓ What Boards Can Do

Acting strategically is difficult. It is easier for boards to think about the issues they know they need to solve right now, that is, the ones on which others—superintendent, community, state government—want action. What boards can do is step back, ask questions, and be persistent.

Here are three actions that are critical:

1. *Take the high road.* Keep thinking and discussing the bigger picture and the longer-range view of the district. Boards get caught up in controversy—immediate issues that must be resolved and community pressure to be appeased. If *you* can't think about what's really important in the long run, who will?

2. *Ask whether things are working in the district.* Don't follow the squeaky wheel. Think about the things that need to be working well and ask about them, anticipating potential problems before they emerge.

3. *Ask whether you should be doing what you're doing as a board.* Is it your place to examine instructional policy or to question school-based practices? Each situation prompts these questions, which should be the subject of explicit discussion among board members and with the superintendent.

Exhibit 6.1 offers questions to consider when evaluating your board's ability to act strategically.

EXHIBIT 6.1
Questions to Consider

Is your board more involved in trying to put out fires than in preparing for the future?

Has your board set clear organizational priorities for the year ahead?

Does your board delay action until an issue becomes urgent or critical?

Do your board meetings tend to focus more on current concerns than on preparing for the future?

At least once a year, does your board ask that the superintendent articulate his or her vision for the school district's future and strategies to realize that vision?

Has your board on occasion evaded responsibility for some important issue facing the school district?

Does your board often discuss where the school district should be headed five or more years into the future?

Within the past year, has your board reviewed the school district's strategies for attaining its long-term goals?

Have there been board meetings where the discussion focused on identifying or overcoming the school district's weaknesses?

Does your board discuss events and trends in the larger environment that may present specific opportunities for your school district?

Does your board make explicit use of the long-range priorities of your school district in dealing with current issues?

Is more than half of your board's time spent in discussions of issues of importance to the school district's long-range future?

Part Two

How to Make School Boards Stronger

Chapter 7

Strengthening the Superintendent-Board Partnership

IF SUPERINTENDENTS ARE ASKED to pinpoint the most contentious part of their job, most will say it's their relationship with their school board. School board members say much the same thing about their relationship with the superintendent. They realize their superintendent can help them function effectively but can also make their lives very difficult. Interviews with board members were often peppered with poignant vignettes:

> Our board-superintendent relationship is different from what I hear about in the other school district. In that district, it's more polarized, more controversial, and with more split votes. The superintendent aligns himself with the board president and that contributes to the problem. The board president is more assertive, takes charge. But there is a withholding of information by one group of board members from another.

Here's another example of an administration being seen as autocratic:

> The superintendent and assistant superintendent are a major frustration to me. The board is irrelevant as far as the administration is concerned. The administrators work around the board. Information is manipulated by the administration. It makes the board ineffective. The administration is not versed in management techniques.

Superintendents are often thought to be withholding information and engineering proposals. When that happens, boards face having to vote on proposals without being able to consider alternatives. More often, however, the lack of partnership takes more subtle turns. Superintendents may do what is required to involve their boards, but they may not put the extra effort into building the board's capacity to function as a full partner. The superintendent may involve the board to gain endorsement for some action and fail to guide them through the consideration of alternative solutions.

The Superintendent as a Partner

Although board members often express frustration with their superintendents, they need effective superintendents. The more competent the superintendent, the more likely a board is to function well. Without the superintendent as a partner, the board may struggle with its role, making decisions that are fragmented or that reflect staff recommendations rather than the board's own perspective. Because board members are mostly part-time volunteers, with neither training in education nor experience with boards and governance, the superintendent is responsible for structuring and organizing the board's work. The superintendent has the expertise, staff, and time to exercise primary influence over the factors that help boards operate effectively. These factors include

The goals, programs, and program accountability measures that define the district's strategic direction

The way problems are defined and alternative solutions are framed for board review

The information and agenda for the board

The way board business is conducted and board members relate in conducting this business

The board's opportunity for training and capacity building

The governance role of the board is, in large part, dependent on the way the board and superintendent relate. If the superintendent ignores the board or coordinates in an arbitrary manner, the board's role becomes compromised.

The Board as a Partner

Superintendents also need to have a partnership with their board. The board and superintendent share a highest-priority interest in the children of their school district and the citizens of their community. Together they face important challenges to current school operations:

They are asked to demonstrate results. In the case of school districts, this means showing that students are learning more.

They are asked to restructure programs to support improved results.

They are increasingly held accountable for cost containment.

They work in communities where confidence in the ability of schools to produce results is diminished, and there is often disagreement regarding the need for programs.

Parents, teachers, and other constituents dispute district policies and procedures, as well as their interpretation.

The superintendent must often take action with less than full community support and in the context of strong state mandates. The superintendent needs the support of an effective board to build community support for actions and to influence state educational policy.

If the board is not a full partner, the superintendent will make decisions knowing that board support may not be strong or consistent. Superintendents may choose to maintain current practice rather than risk the lack of board support for stronger action.

The Meaning of Partnership

Partnership means that the superintendent and board work together in forming and achieving the goals and strategic direction for the district. It means that the superintendent and the board, in concert, frame problems that are critical to the district and pursue solutions. It means information is shared openly to support defining problems and seeking answers.[1]

The concept of partnership departs from the traditional board–chief executive model of governance and management. Common wisdom has suggested a separation of policy and administration: the board deals with policy issues, and the superintendent runs the school district on a day-to-day basis. The board-superintendent partnership does not contradict this concept. It simply places an emphasis on goals and outcomes for the district and acknowledges that the relative roles of boards and superintendents must be fluid, depending on the district and the situation. This is particularly true in times when board support is required, not only in the conceptualization of change but in its implementation.

When the superintendent and the board decide they will work together, they build a common view of how the district should change. Then when the superintendent does make changes, he or she has the board's support.

The Risks for Superintendents

For the superintendent, thinking of the board as a true partner can carry risks as well as rewards, given the power the board has. It hires the superintendent. And it can fire the superintendent who runs too far afoul of its wishes. Thinking of such an employer—particularly one that is as politically motivated as boards are—as a true partner can be problematic. A superintendent must be skillful and diplomatic in any effort to develop a partnership.

Another risk that true partnership carries for superintendents is the possibility of having to partner with opponents—possibly with very outspoken critics of the administration. In most districts board membership changes every few years. New members, elected on a platform critical of current practice, may not support the superintendent. And the board does have the authority to act in ways that are contrary to the superintendent's recommendations. This is a difficult, sometimes politically untenable position for a superintendent to be in.

How Boards Can Reduce Risk

The board must create a working climate that reduces the risk for the superintendent and paves the way for true partnership. This requires establishing expectations, providing support, and holding the superintendent accountable. It requires developing consensus around a vision of the district's future and understanding the superintendent's job.

The board, along with the superintendent, must develop a clear idea of how the partnership will work and define the mutual obligations of superintendent and board. This view must take into consideration a realistic picture of the pressures facing the superintendent. The board's consistent support in the face of community criticism is particularly important.

Boards should focus on what matters, develop an action plan to best accomplish what matters, and forge a relationship with the superintendent that supports that accomplishment.[2]

Focus on what matters.

Board members should ask, What needs to be accomplished in our district? This is the basic question. Next they should ask, Where do we as a district want to be?, How will we get there?, and How do we as a board contribute to that process?

The board should try to answer these questions. But they are hard, and answering them takes time; it takes organized discussion—quite apart from the pressure of daily board business. In a partnership, the superintendent will set the stage in consultation with the board: it's a planning process, with collaborative roles for superintendent and board, and with explicit attention to how the board can add value. The superintendent, with board input, will frame answers for board review and modification.

Because superintendents may vary in their desire and capacity to partner, the board must be prepared to provide its own focus to answer these questions. The way planning is introduced, its structure, the information provided to the board, and the process of board consideration are all-important in determining whether the board can shape the answers to determine district goals and its own role.

There are many constructive approaches. What is important is that jointly, board and superintendent identify the most important issues facing the district. They must say to themselves: If we solve this problem, we should improve student learning. Then they should begin to explore what the board should do to help solve the problem.

My interviews with board members illustrate the focus on what matters. Here's an example of a superintendent and board working collaboratively to focus:

> The process of setting the agenda is an open process. There is a weekly packet of materials from the superintendent. The superintendent will talk individually with each board member and then fashion a plan to gain acceptance. He has a vision of what he wants, but it doesn't always match what individual board members want. He floats ideas to see what will happen. He's good at working with the board.

Here's another example of a board being focused in its discussion:

> The board has a good relationship with the superintendent. The board sits with the superintendent and his directors to discuss all issues. The board gets input and truly discusses issues rather than being told at the last minute what action is recommended. The superintendent is visible. He listens to what school people are saying. He is not dictatorial.

Develop and implement an action plan.

Board members should consider these questions: Who does what to be sure that those items of highest importance are considered and action is taken? and How can we be sure the board is properly involved? How can the board add value?

This is where the model for board effectiveness (see Exhibit 1, Preface) is particularly helpful. Whatever course of action, the board must function effectively to ensure successful execution. It is this effective functioning that can best build a partnership with the superintendent.

Following the outline of the Model for School Board Effectiveness, here's what the effective board must do and what it must expect of its superintendent:

- *Make decisions.* Board members must be sure they are receiving the most relevant information on the most important issues and that their discussion of these issues is deliberate, objective, and open. The board must ensure that the level of discussion addresses the value differences among board members that interfere with building consensus. The board should expect the superintendent to develop the information and frame discussion to accomplish these objectives, structuring the agenda to focus on what is important. The partnership is fulfilled as the board and superintendent work collaboratively to ensure that this takes place, sharing the value placed on appropriate discussion of important issues.

- *Function as a group.* The board must understand and agree on norms and operating values that enable its members to function as a cohesive group. Such a group respects its members and exercises leadership through focusing group energy on the important tasks at hand. The board should expect the superintendent to help articulate norms and values and structure situations that enable the board to become more effective in its group functioning. The partnership is fulfilled as the board and superintendent share in planning and monitoring this group functioning.

- *Exercise authority.* The board must be independent of the superintendent. The board should expect the superintendent to allow and encourage this independent action. The partnership occurs when board and superintendent understand and respectfully discuss their differences and when the discussion frames these differences and their rationale, forming the basis for the board's independent action.

- *Relate to the community.* The board must ensure community input and understanding with appropriate information flow. The board should expect the superintendent to structure and execute this flow of discussion and information. Superintendent and board in partnership collaboratively develop and execute plans for relating to the community.

- *Work toward board improvement.* The board must assess its own competence and plan for improvement. The board should expect the superintendent to support this process with structure and insight into board development. As partners, board and superintendent jointly assess their performance and work for improvement.

• *Act strategically.* The board and superintendent plan, organize, and evaluate the purposes, programs, and operation of the school district. Typically, the board gives input, monitors, and gives feedback, ensuring that the issues board members consider critical are addressed. The superintendent structures and carries out this strategic planning process, involving the board in shaping and evaluating the district's strategic direction. Board and superintendent in partnership define and execute the process collaboratively; they define roles to ensure the best result.

Forge a relationship with the superintendent.

School board member should ask themselves, How can the partnership be established and maintained? Boards tend to rely on superintendent leadership to build a strong relationship, and the best superintendents can often be quite successful in doing so. But the board itself should take strong action with the perspective of helping the superintendent to be successful in leading the district. Here's how:

• *Choose the right person.* The initial selection process is all-important. The board must be clear about its expectations of the superintendent. The board should explore with candidates the potential board-superintendent relationship. As board members described in their interviews, the search for a new superintendent provides an important opportunity for the board to consider its vision for the district and its concept of board operations. The Model for Board Effectiveness provides a framework for board self-assessment and for establishing the requirements for a new superintendent that will support a strong partnership.

• *Set expectations.* Spend time with the superintendent, talking through how the board will operate and what the superintendent's role should be. The expectations derived from the six elements of an effective board are a good starting place. Other expectations will come out of the strategic directions for the district. The process of setting expectations should be mutual and ongoing.

• *Evaluate progress.* The board should evaluate the relationship—through self-evaluation and evaluation of the superintendent. The evaluation should be multifaceted: formal and informal, periodic and ongoing, programmatic and interpersonal. The board's evaluation should be mutual, with the board evaluating itself and the superintendent and the superintendent evaluating him- or herself and the board (see Chapter Nine). The board and superintendent should establish a comparable set of processes for superintendent evaluation. The superintendent should complete a self-assessment, and the board should formally assess the superintendent with reference to that self-assessment and the established expectations.. The board should informally monitor the process, giving frequent performance feedback to the superintendent. And the superintendent should demonstrate efforts toward self-development. The spirit of partnership calls for a mutual sharing and critiquing.

• *Provide opportunities for communication.* The interviews with school board members highlight the value of good communication between board and superintendent and vice versa. Communication must be based on trust; open discussion of what is really important and how compromise can be achieved should be encouraged. The tension between political and policy agendas make this difficult but all the more important. Board and superintendent must support each board member and the superintendent in trying to serve constituents—staff and community, individuals, and groups—while placing the greatest importance on providing high-quality education for all students.

How can the board foster this communication? Some possibilities are to

Provide opportunities for frank discussion—for example, retreats and meetings where no actions are required.

Use outside facilitators to help examine issues and suggest solutions.

Use the board president to meet regularly and frequently with the superintendent and to communicate with board members.

Often the biggest barrier to communication is the failure of the board to recognize that partnership requires the board to consider the superintendent's needs. The board can act as a support for the superintendent, providing encouragement and perspective. This is often done in individual conversation, and the board president is typically the one to represent the board in providing this support.

Superintendent Steps Toward Partnership

Superintendents should promote board development, build partnerships with their board, and focus attention on what matters most. The focus on the board here is deliberate. Interviews with superintendents would provide a rich account of their effective actions in establishing the superintendent-board partnership. Such information would demonstrate that when the superintendent does exercise leadership, an informed and effective board is most likely to realize an opportunity for partnership.

Promote board development.

Board members begin their work with little formal training or experience. Those interviewed often cited the superintendent as the key resource person to help them learn the job. This recommendation calls for superintendents to perform this mentoring role deliberately and systematically, taking primary responsibility for tapping board and community resources in helping board members to learn their jobs.

Chapter Nine outlines a process of systematic board development; the barriers to its implementation are considerable. For example, boards often lack time, experience, and a sense that board development is important. The superintendent should provide expertise and leadership to a board as it considers its own evaluation and opportunities for improvement.

Build partnerships.

Building a partnership depends on shared goals and a commitment to work together. It is formed and maintained by planning and evaluation. It is supported by communication, information, agenda, interpersonal interactions, and ground rules for conducting business. The superintendent should structure processes by which the board functions.

Focus on what matters.

Boards often focus attention on the trivial, routine decisions that are a part of everyday district operation. The superintendent can fashion the agenda so the important issues become the focus of board attention. The superintendent can take each item in the board's list of actions and ask how he or she can promote their accomplishment.

Conclusion

Although the board-superintendent relationship is fraught with peril, it is certainly possible for a strong, supportive partnership to develop. Good management techniques, consistent information flow, and shared goals are the keys to forging a solid connection that benefits the entire school community. Just how a better information flow can be achieved is the subject of the next chapter.

Chapter 8

Getting the Best Information

INFORMATION AND AGENDA contribute significantly to a school board's capacity to be effective and are central tools in forging a board-superintendent partnership. Specifically, information is central to some critically important questions:

What issues, out of so many, should find their way to the agenda and thus occupy the board's attention?

Who makes this decision?

What information about these issues should be selected for board consideration? Who should select it? How should it be selected?

How can it best be conveyed?

In a more general sense, information is *support*. It helps boards make good decisions and plans, providing a rational, objective basis for understanding and action. But it is also a powerful *influence*. It shapes agendas, identifying and justifying issues for consideration. It frames choices, pointing toward one decision over another. Information affects trust and contributes to the relationship between board and superintendent. It is the tangible evidence of open, honest communication.

Board member interviews reflect their awareness of this essential interconnection. Here are several examples of board members commenting on the importance of information and the superintendent's role:

> The superintendent keeps board members very well informed. . . . When the board comes for the meeting, information must be available. The superintendent keeps the board informed about everything. It's a constant communication process.

In other instances, members cite the problems caused by *not* having information:

> In the past some board members were privy to information that other board members didn't have. I stressed the importance of working together as a board as a whole, not as individuals.

But boards rarely consider systematically and deliberately the information they need and the form it should take. When they do, the consideration brings them to the critical questions of priorities and communication. They discover that information and agenda direct their energies and significantly influence their effectiveness.[1]

Regulating the Flow of Information

There is—or should be—a planned flow of information for board decision making. Usually the superintendent decides what information the board should receive. To make that decision, the superintendent gets input from the board, from individual board members, from state and federal education agencies, and from constituent groups at the local and state level, any of which may provide information directly. The choice of information is driven by the circumstances of particular agenda items and their requirements or by whether items are of interest to particular constituents. Usually, information is in the form of background information about a decision to be made by the board. Sometimes it comes from the community—from community members' testimony about their views on key issues. Seldom does the board deliberately devise a way to obtain the information it needs.

Board members and board observers are often critical of the amount, perspective, quality, balance, and level of detail of the information they receive. There may be more than they can absorb and not enough effort to highlight what board members need to know, which makes it difficult to determine what's really important. Materials provided may be selectively biased, making it hard to balance alternatives or understand the core issues.

Jay Lorsch, in his excellent article "Empowering the Board," emphasizes knowledge:[2] "Knowledge is the appropriate word here instead of the more frequently used information because the directors' real problem is not lack of information but its content and context. . . . Boards . . . really need to understand the material presented so they can participate more effectively."

Board members are confronted with information in a form that often makes it difficult for them to obtain the knowledge needed for effective board action. Information may come from different sources, and the quality of the information is difficult to ascertain, as illustrated by this school board interviewee's comment:

> As a new board member, functioning in the job is difficult. You are unsure about other people on the board. You want to find out their strengths and weaknesses before playing your hand. You don't want to be overly aggressive but want the board to know you are an equal member. The hardest part is how to find out who has the information you want and what information exists.

The board's work in distilling information into useful knowledge is made even more difficult by the informal network of communications each board member has with his constituencies. The volume of letters, calls, and e-mails, while helping board members understand community views, makes the distillation of what's important even more difficult and emphasizes the political perspective on issues that may need rational analysis.

The net effect is that information is often used poorly, hindering rather than helping boards in their efforts to make wise decisions. Members feel the need to review information carefully, and this review can place excessive demands on their time. The focus on this information can also divert attention from issues and information of greater consequence. It can even represent an attempt by staff to manipulate board action through directing attention to a biased portion of the information important to a particular subject. Using information effectively and efficiently requires careful attention to what information is provided, how that is decided, and who offers it.

Understanding the Role of Information

Information supports the school board in the performance of its essential responsibilities. It focuses the board's attention where the board can provide greatest value to the district; it shapes the effectiveness of its work; it contributes to the quality of the board's working relationships.

The information required is linked to board responsibilities, to the six elements of school board effectiveness, and to essential board relationships.

Relates to responsibilities.

The information that is important to a school board should relate to the fundamental responsibilities of that board. These responsibilities, as presented in the introductory chapter, suggest that boards need information on

Mission, values, goals, program, organization, planning, standards, accountability, performance monitoring

Budget, curriculum, and personnel

Contracts, collaborative projects

Crises that endanger individuals or create strong community views

The problem with this list is that it covers just about everything. The challenge, discussed later in the chapter, is how to pick relevant information from this universe.

Fulfills the elements of effectiveness.

In the first six chapters, I outlined the six areas for effective school board action—components in the model for board effectiveness. Here's how information supports and shapes each of the six areas:

1. *Making decisions.* Identical information should be available to all board members. It should highlight the important areas where decisions are needed. For critical areas, it should provide the information essential to deliberate, objective decisions with consideration of alternatives. It should surface arguments and counterarguments that give a balanced view of issues under consideration.

2. *Functioning as a group.* The information required for making decisions supports group functioning. The open, objective use of information builds respect and trust. Norms for effective group functioning include those governing how information generated and provided.

3. *Exercising authority.* Where the board must take initiative and, in some instances, differ from the superintendent in recommendations, the board must obtain information independent of the superintendent, or ideally, through the superintendent's commitment to provide information that may be counter to his point of view.

4. *Connecting to the community.* Information from community to board is critical to effective decision making and to building a close board-community relationship of trust. The board also becomes a provider of information in seeking community understanding of board action on important issues.

5. *Working toward board improvement.* Chapter Nine outlines specific information that can be useful as a board considers its own operation and ways it can improve. Multiple sources of information can be particularly

important here, as the board needs objective, third-party assessment of its performance and the perceptions of constituents.

6. *Acting strategically.* Information is critical in understanding the context of district operation and considering what issues are critical and how to address them and assess progress.

Strengthens essential relationships.

The board must seek and consider information from its constituencies. This includes information from the district through the superintendent and staff, as well as from community groups, government agencies, and other key opinion leaders.

The role of seeking and considering information in strengthening relationships adds difficulty to the management of board information for effective action. It is hard to exclude information that may be of lower priority to the board but of high priority to constituent groups.

Establishing Information Priorities

Working with their superintendents, boards should deliberately plan for receiving information. The plan should consider the kinds of information, the level of detail, and its conveyance. This is complex but important; it is often ignored.

There is typically a tension between items of immediate concern, particularly to specific constituencies or other collaborating organizations, and those of long-term interest—implementing plans and meeting standards. A planned board information system provides for the crisis without losing the long-range view.

Information is provided for different circumstances. Tracking progress against plans and standards requires systematic, periodic scheduled information. Briefing for a fast-developing set of events requires immediate information and interaction.

Information is also provided for different reasons. Some supports systematic progress toward predetermined goals. Some ensures board understanding of events that occur in the district and community.

Each district must determine what information is important. Ultimately, the board must take responsibility for its information. Because the selection of information influences the way the board spends time and how it views the issues it should address, it must make the fundamental decisions about the kind and form of information it wants. If the board and the superintendent enjoy mutual trust, the superintendent and staff can frame the ideas for board approval.

Here are key points to consider:

• *The design process is as important as the result.* What information is needed? When is it needed and in what form? By asking these questions, the board is planning its priorities and the standards for measuring progress. An astute board will devote time to the process as a device for concrete strategic planning. Butler discovered this in his project on *Board Information Systems.*[3]

> The process of developing a board information system can be every bit as important as the system it produces. Many board members who have been through it have greatly appreciated the process itself—quite apart from the resulting report formats. The process can help the board to clarify its thinking about its own role vis-à-vis staff, its overall structure and work style, and perhaps most importantly, about institutional mission and how to assure its achievement. Improving board information, in other words, serves as an excellent point of entry for meaningful introspection and dialogue within the board and with staff on a broad range of important subjects.

• *The superintendent should participate as partner.* The partnership of board and superintendent suggests joint planning of board information requirements. Ideally, the superintendent can bring to the board a schedule of key agenda items and the information that the board will need to support decisions about these items. The process of board-superintendent discussion will help focus board attention on issues of highest priority and will refine the types of information the board receives. The superintendent has the best access to information. The design process provides a basis for mutual understanding of what is needed. The board should hold the superintendent accountable for providing the information.

• *The board information requirements should vary by purpose.* I have focused on information for board planning, monitoring, assessing progress, being fiscally accountable, and other critical decision-making activities. These are basic board responsibilities. But the board uses information for other purposes, and the information design should encompass these as well.

Identifying Information Categories

Following are some useful distinctions among categories of information:

Long-term, short-term, and *crisis.* The board must know about day-to-day events in the operation of the schools that affect the safety and welfare of students and staff, the condition of property, the fiscal health of the district, and the legal status of board and district actions. Circumstances may require immediate communication. However, in many cases whether issues have shorter or longer time frames for resolution, information can be planned in advance.

Public and *confidential.* Most information is a matter of public record. However, some personnel, contractual, and legal information is not.

Central to decision making and background and *context.* Some information is useful because it helps board members understand trends and issues; other information presents alternative recommendations with rationale.

Anticipated and *unanticipated issues.* For some issues, information can be planned because the issues occur periodically. For example, budget approval is an annual action.

Input to board and *outflow from board.* Some information is designed to inform the board. Other information is to inform the public, media, and governmental agencies about board and district activities.

Community focus and *district focus.* The input and outflow may be to receive the advice of superintendent and district and to give advice and feedback. It may be to understand staff and public concerns and perceptions, and to provide information leading to staff and community understanding.

Compliance and *development.* Some information is a formal response to state and federal agencies to meet accountability requirements; other information is for local district program development or monitoring purposes.

These differences should help boards decide which means of conveying information are appropriate. The timing, breadth of dissemination, audience, type of input, complexity of information, confidentiality, purpose (compliance versus developmental), and other factors, should determine how information is actually conveyed. Most board information is communicated through written reports or presentations; hearings and workshops provide opportunity for broader input.

The organization of information and its display can add significantly to the ease with which information is understood. Developing a board information plan should include attention to design tools and principles.

Larry Butler, in his unpublished handbook *Board Information Systems*, demonstrates the power of this approach and of the insights a board achieves through the process of determining how to display important information for enhanced understanding.[4]

There should be clear rules governing the use of information. Because it is the board, not its members as individuals, that has legal authority, the board as a unit should decide what information is important and approve the design of the board information system. Each board member should have timely access to the same information. The process by which individual board members seek information should ensure that all board members and the superintendent are aware of these actions and that they do not go outside the normal channels to seek or give out information on their own.

Assessing and Planning an Information System

Using the previous discussion, board members and their superintendent should examine the information received and ask the following questions about it:[5]

1. Does it have a governance perspective? Does the information help the board understand issues that are central board concerns? These include the district's goals and programs, the degree to which they are accomplished, priorities and plans, the changes outside the district that may influence its future direction, institutional liability, the amount and distribution of resources, community and interagency relationships, and contractual matters. Is the information focused on what is done and why, without undue emphasis on how it is accomplished?

2. Does it have strategic relevance? Does it have an impact on the long-term strengthening of the district in providing educational services to children?

3. Is it moderate in volume? More information is not the answer. School board members complain about the volume of information they receive. Having all the information is unnecessary and virtually impossible. Is the information selected to best enable the board to make the decisions required?

4. Is it appropriate in level of detail? It should neither be too general nor too detailed. It should give perspective appropriate to the board actions required, with opportunity for requesting and receiving additional detail where necessary.

5. Is it for the full board? Conscientious individual board members, often with time and curiosity, may wish to probe more deeply into specific issues. Their requests for information may skew the energies of staff in providing information and distort the degree of information appropriate for the board. Is the information balanced and focused on the important work of the board?

6. Is the board time required moderate? Board members are not full-time employees of the district and must use their limited time efficiently. The amount and format of the information they receive significantly affects their efficiency.

7. Is the information grounded in objective analysis? Performance can be judged based on predetermined and objective indicators. Decisions can be framed by analysis of alternative actions. Where information is anecdotal and episodic, it is less useful and does not fully inform to enable effective board action.

8. Is it an adequate guide for action? The information must be framed for assessing issues and considering alternative decisions. It needs the context of historic trends, matched with objectives or standards and comparative analysis. It needs an analysis of recommended action with sufficient justification.

Asking the Difficult Questions

There are no easy answers to these questions; consensus on what information should be provided won't be easy to reach. Here are some of the more troublesome questions:

How can we draw the line on what information we need to make decisions? You may wish to consider three layers of information: a summary of what is essential, the information you should review, and the back-up information that is available but you need not review. For example, the superintendent, perhaps with a designated board member, may highlight the changes in the new English curriculum, identifying those areas that are most controversial while the curriculum itself is available for review by those desiring to do so.

What about the letters, phone calls, e-mails, and other communications we receive individually from constituents? Individual board members must decide how to handle their relationships with constituents. For example, board members can decide to handle all calls through a board office, or they may feel they should answer calls at home. Some board members summarize the content of these interactions to share with all members. These decisions are important and have an impact on the board's image of responsiveness. The question is worth discussing in the general board review of information.

This advice is helpful for longer-term planning, but how do we handle information in time of crisis? In crisis, information changes faster; board members are challenged and lobbied, and the media are often involved; constituents and staff may have strongly held viewpoints. But members must have information to make good decisions, so ways to get it without being overwhelmed should be sorted out periodically. For example, there could be a periodic e-mail or telephone call to brief each board member; the superintendent or the board president could send the message. Or there could be an agreement to keep the superintendent or board president informed of individual board member activities, with summaries sent to the board. The principle of full information, provided to each board member on a timely basis, is all-important.

Who speaks for the board? The board and board members are asked to comment on issues. The district submits press releases, and superintendent and board representatives are interviewed by the media. How well the board comes across to the public contributes to board effectiveness, so guidelines should be established. Board members should be clear when they are speaking as individuals; they should not speak as representatives of the board unless so designated. If board members debate differences in public, they make ultimate consensus more difficult—even while they contribute to public debate about important issues.

Conclusion

A sound superintendent-board partnership supported by the right governance information sets the stage for a board to build its capacity to function effectively. The next chapter addresses the specific steps a board can take in its efforts toward self-improvement.

Chapter 9

Engaging in Board Development

SCHOOL BOARDS, like most public and not-for-profit boards, tend to do the things that are required or expected, whether by law, by administrative practice, or by community demand. Yet the changes in our society and educational reform initiatives challenge boards to function effectively and to provide leadership for the changes needed in our public education system.

Earlier chapters have shown that board members know what it takes to be effective. So why don't they always act accordingly? Can boards learn to be effective? The clear evidence from experts and school board members shows that a developmental model of a board working together is central to improving board effectiveness. A group of experts, convened to discuss school board development, concluded that "boards need to understand adaptive work; they need to build a culture that allows civil discourse and guides how they behave toward each other."[1]

Interviews with experts suggest that boards also need time together, preferably in a retreat setting apart from the regular agenda of their meetings. They need this time to discuss their values, vision, and means of working together. As one of the experts interviewed, consultant Vic Cottrell, says:

> There are four conditions for an effective board: it must develop a collective vision; in spite of diversity, its members should communicate in an honest forthright way; the board members should agree on reasonable processes for making decisions; and the board should agree on how it will measure its own performance. To become an effective board, its members must agree to periodically spend time together without a specific task or agenda. They should use the time to get to know each

other; to explore their perceptions of what brings meaning to their board work; to dream about what they could do for the district; to consider what leadership they need; and to agree on how they should behave among themselves.

The Concept of Board Development

Board development should provide a collective and comprehensive experience. But typical board training is in the form of short, single-topic courses in board responsibilities and educational policy, offered to individual board members from a number of districts.[2] *Ideal board development* is a sustained program for a full board, with an integrated approach to topics and an emphasis on self-assessment, basic purposes, and board functioning. The end results are an understanding and commitment to shared purposes and effective board performance.

Self-Assessment.

Self-assessment is particularly important for board development because it frames the discussion of purpose and function and motivates performance. By looking at its own operation, a board has the opportunity to discuss key issues of purpose and operation:

What are we accomplishing? As a board, are we accomplishing what we should be?

Is our district improving as it should? Are we helping the district in its efforts to improve?

How are we functioning? How are we doing in each of the six areas of effective board activity: making decisions, functioning as a group, exercising authority, connecting to the community, working toward board improvement, and acting strategically?

Are there issues that keep us from performing our work effectively?

Discussion of purpose.

The very act of self-examination leads to a discussion of purpose and thus focuses on improvement. Self-assessment leads to setting board expectations and making an effort to perform according to these expectations. And the discussion of purpose leads to shared understanding and commitment to accomplishment. To reach this understanding, board members need time to reflect on what they do and to talk with each other about things they believe are most important for the district to achieve. They must ask key questions:

What do we, as a board, need to accomplish? Why?

Where are we headed? Where is our district headed?

How can we help the district get there?

Assessment of board functioning.

Given its limited time and energy, a board must focus on adding value to its district in pursuit of better education. But it's not enough for a board to follow an agenda and respond to community concerns. The board should find out how well it is doing. When boards are systematic and deliberate in discussing their own operation, they emphasize the performance of the board as a unit, not just as a collection of individuals.

How Boards Can Improve

Boards can take three essential action steps toward their own improvement:

1. *Conduct a self-assessment.* This is a well-defined, one-time action that provides basic information for boards to use in considering their own value and operation. It takes a current information picture of the board and becomes a baseline for board discussion of its performance. The outcome should be a set of goals for self-improvement. Self-assessment typically involves a questionnaire and interviews. Because the first part of this book has presented a framework for self-assessment of board effectiveness, this section presents a questionnaire and process to use in conjunction with this framework.

2. *Implement monitoring.* This is a continuing process, building on self-assessment, which periodically considers how well the board is accomplishing its goals for self-improvement.

3. *Engage in systematic development.* This is a comprehensive set of activities encompassing self-assessment and monitoring; it builds in a retreat activity to consider the results of the self-assessment and plan the monitoring process; it includes planning and executing the process by which the board considers opportunities for improvement. The process itself leads to improved understanding and board functioning.

The following section describes the three essential actions in more detail.

Action One: Conduct Self-Assessment

Take stock of where the board is: how it works, how it does business. As this book demonstrates, board members generally know what it is to be effective. But they rarely talk about it and often don't practice what they know. They fail to assess their areas of agreement and disagreement.

As a start, a board must have a framework or template to use in determining its effectiveness. It must agree that this framework is a good one to use (at least as a starting point, not necessarily as a definitive model) and agree that self-assessment is worth the effort.

One possible set of actions is as follows:

• *Agree on purpose.* The first step is to consider and reach agreement on the purpose of and approach to such a process. Typically, the objective is to take an independent look at how the board is functioning and to use this information as the basis for discussion on areas for possible improvement. The superintendent and board president, or a subcommittee of the board, may create a brief proposal for board review.

Are there particular issues the board wants to address? For example, there might be one of the following:

A breach of confidentiality

A negative, impatient tone in board discussion

The desire to consider how the board can get at broader issues of curriculum or community understanding

A need to integrate new board members into the operation of the board

A planning effort in the district, opening up an opportunity for the board to participate through its own planning

Often, specific issues prompt the board to feel an urgency about the self-assessment process: the selection of a new superintendent, the need for approval of a referendum for increased taxes, the redistricting of schools, the revision of program or school organization, to name a few. Boards are more likely to consider self-assessment when individual board members hold strong and disparate views, community groups are pushing for particular solutions, and the board urgently needs a decision.

• *Develop a proposal.* After agreement is reached on purpose and approach, one person or group (superintendent, board president, board subcommittee, outside citizens group, or consultant) develops a proposal for self-assessment for the board's review and approval. The proposal should address the general issue of data and process. First, what information should be gathered on assessment of current practices? A self-assessment questionnaire and separate interviews with individual board members are useful tools. The board may wish to consider the perceptions of staff and community members.

• *Decide who collects information.* Next, decide whether to use an outside expert or facilitator to help collect and evaluate the information. An outside expert can assist the board in its discussion by independently assessing the information. A facilitator may enable the board to organize its discussion as openly and candidly as possible, which is particularly important if the relationship among board members is part of the assessment. Sometimes the expert and facilitator can be the same person.

• *Decide who will process information.* Now consider how the board will process the information. Someone (an outside consultant, expert or facilitator, the superintendent, the board president, or a board subcommittee, for example) should review the material and develop an agenda of discussion issues, perhaps in consultation with individual board members.

• *Decide how information will be discussed.* The question of how the information will be discussed comes next. Should it be an agenda item of a regular board meeting, or is there a need for a special session? How much time should be reserved for the discussion? What are the expected results? Will there be a series of recommendations for improvement?

• *Decide how the public will be involved.* Should the board publicize its decision to undertake a self-assessment? Should the community have input? Should a report of the results be available or distributed to the community?

Select the process.

The process I recommend begins with administering the self-assessment questionnaire that appears in Appendix B. Individual board member responses create an initial set of data. (This questionnaire reflects the Model for School Board Effectiveness developed in Chapters One through Six.) Board members can understand and interpret the results of their self-assessment by referring to the model.

If desired, open-ended questions may supplement the questionnaire. For example, a board might ask its members to list the primary issues the board should consider during the next year or to outline their views on the norms that should govern board action. Individual interviews with board members, which uncover their specific concerns and ideas, may also supplement the questionnaire. An outside consultant, an individual board member, or the superintendent might conduct these interviews.

Gather information.

Each board member receives the questionnaire and information on the Model for School Board Effectiveness, reviews the materials with appropriate opportunity to ask questions, and completes the questionnaire. To enhance independent perspectives, board members should initially complete the surveys without consultation. Every member should complete the questionnaire, even anonymously if desired.

Typically, the school district distributes and collects the surveys. However, the National School Boards Association through its webpage (http://www.nsba.org) has the model and questionnaire on-line and accessible to board members through its Resource Exchange Network. Also, Holland, Blackmon & Associates can score and display the information.[3]

Synthesize results.

A superintendent, board president, independent consultant, or other designated individual can tabulate and analyze the results of the questionnaire. A simple tabulation will provide a display of the answers for each question. For ease in discussion, these can be organized by each of the six areas of activity. These responses suggest strengths and areas for board improvement. They can be analyzed to frame a series of questions for the board to answer about its own activity. Exhibits 9.1 and 9.2 illustrate the typical responses of a district and likely questions for board review and discussion.

The quality and objectivity of this analysis is critical. Focusing on the right questions is key. The use of an outside expert or facilitator to assist in this analysis may be particularly important.

Consider implications.

In this step, the board considers the results, using the questionnaire responses and analysis as the basis for discussion. This discussion should address at least four types of questions:

How well are we doing?

Where do we need improvement?

What could we do differently?

What is our commitment for the future?

This discussion should be systematic and deliberate. Boards may want to use an outside facilitator for this step to enhance the exploration of important, sometimes sensitive, areas where improvement may be needed.

EXHIBIT 9.1

BOARD SELF-ASSESSMENT QUESTIONNAIRE:
Sample School District Summary Responses

Format adapted from "Assessment of Board Performance," Holland, Blackmon & Assocs., Inc., Athens, Georgia, February, 1998, unpublished report. Used by permission of Holland, Blackmon & Associates, Inc.

This chart displays the responses of a sample school district of nine members to the self-assessment questionnaire (Appendix B), comparing their responses to those responses that might be anticipated using the Model for School Board Effectiveness. This gives a rough estimate of the degree to which the board follows the model in its current work.

   Note: This is not an assessment of the board. It provides a basis for discussion of the differences between the individual board score and the model score.

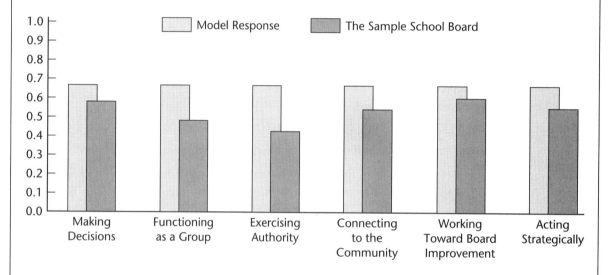

MAKING DECISIONS. Boards describe a decision-making process with a variety of distinctive characteristics. It is a rational process, informed by data and full discussion. Members maintain flexibility and objectivity when considering the merits of alternative courses of action. The process works toward a consensus of views, rather than a majority vote.

FUNCTIONING AS A GROUP. Interviewees describe a shared respect and trust that recognizes the contribution of each board member. The effective board has many characteristics of well-functioning groups: a feeling of cohesiveness and of working together, shared goals and values, leadership within the board (often the board president), and a shared understanding and agreement on operating rules.

EXERCISING AUTHORITY. Board members speak of their effective activities in the context of the superintendent's recommendations and actions. There is support for the chief executive but a sensitivity about not being a rubber-stamp board. Board members cite examples of effectiveness where they initiated actions, overruled the superintendent, or withstood the pressure of staff, community, and government.

CONNECTING TO THE COMMUNITY. Board members cite their actions in maintaining a multifaceted relationship with the community. This relationship includes informal conversation and structured input from the community as well as board presentations to the community. Board members serve as a conduit between the school district and community.

WORKING TOWARD BOARD IMPROVEMENT. Interviewees discuss activities that help new members understand their responsibilities. They describe actions that include reflection on and adjustment of board responsibilities and authority. They seek outside assistance and cultivate leadership and membership on the board.

ACTING STRATEGICALLY. Board members discuss and resolve issues that are central to assisting children to learn. They plan systematically and long term, taking into consideration the needs and concerns of internal and external constituents, balancing substantive and political realities. They match plans against results. They organize responsibilities and authority between superintendent and board, adjusting for strengths and weaknesses.

Boards should review each of the six areas of activity. The discussion should celebrate areas where the board functions well.

The ideal outcome of this process is a plan for board improvement and a commitment from the board to implement the plan. This leads to a monitoring process that adds continuity.

A Self-Assessment Example

For a typical board, members complete the questionnaire (see Appendix B). The responses for the seventy-three questions are clustered by the six areas of effective activity and then compared with that of an "ideal" board, following the model presented in the first six chapters of this book. The average response is compared with this ideal, with a percentage of ideal response assigned. Exhibit 9.1 illustrates this analysis for the sample board.

Using this exhibit, findings and issues might include the following:

In our responses in the category Exercising Authority, we deviate most from the ideal responses of the model. Why is this?

Do we disagree with the principles set forth in the chapter on exercising authority (Chapter Three) or the survey questions clustered in this activity area?

Do our responses suggest that we should assess how our board exercises authority?

EXHIBIT 9.2

ACTIVITY AREA #3: Exercising Authority (Board Response by Item)

Format adapted from "Assessment of Board Performance," Holland, Blackmon & Assocs., Inc., Athens, Georgia, February, 1998, unpublished report. Used by permission of Holland, Blackmon & Associates, Inc.

The following chart reports the sample board's responses to the items on the *Board Self-Assessment Questionnaire.* The complete analysis would include responses to all six dimensions of the Model for School Board Effectiveness.

	Strongly Agree	Agree	Disagree	Strongly Disagree
7. Usually the board and superintendent advocate the same actions.	1	3	4	1
14. The board will sharply question certain administrative proposals, requiring the superintendent to reconsider the recommendation.	0	4	5	0
15. The board is always involved in decisions that are important to the future of education in our district.	1	3	5	0
35. *The board will often persuade the superintendent to change his mind about recommendations.	1	2	4	2
43. The board often requests additional information before making a decision.	1	3	5	1
45. The board often discusses its role in district management.	0	3	6	0
48. *Recommendations from the administration are usually accepted with little questioning.	2	5	2	0
51. The board president and superintendent confer so that differences of opinion are identified.	1	2	4	2
57. We are not a "rubber-stamp" board.	0	2	4	3
63. This board often acts independent of the superintendent's recommendations.	1	1	6	1
67. The board is outspoken in its views about programs.	0	1	6	2
71. *The board will reverse its position based on pressure from the community.	2	5	1	1

Items that have an asterisk (*) describe behaviors that are not typical of effective boards. Strong agreement on these items is a sign of ineffectiveness.

Should we consider these same questions in other categories such as Functioning as a Group where our responses also deviate from the ideal responses of the model?

In Working Toward Board Improvement, our responses most closely resemble that of the model. What are we doing right? Does it help?

For each of the six areas of the model, as shown in Exhibit 9.1, there is additional, more detailed information describing the responses to each of the seventy-three questions related to that area of activity. For example, the category Exercising Authority has a rating based on the answers to twelve of the seventy-three questions. These responses are shown in Exhibit 9.2. (For a district whose board members complete the questionnaire, there would be six such responses, one for each of the six activity categories in which responses are summarized in Exhibit 9.1.)

Boards can glean more detailed information by looking at the distribution of answers to each question. For example, based on the first question, the analysis in the area of Exercising Authority might find that

Board members perceive that the board and superintendent do not usually advocate the same actions (question 7, Exhibit 9.2).

Board members usually do not question administrative proposals (question 48, Exhibit 9.2).

The board is not outspoken in its views about programs (question 67, Exhibit 9.2).

This may suggest a series of questions for board discussion, such as the following:

Do we need to change our working relationship with the superintendent?

Is it related to the way we consider superintendent recommendations?

Do we need to be clearer about our expectations of the superintendent?

Are we as supportive as we should be?

What changes should we make in the way we work with the superintendent?

A final section of the analysis for board discussion might ask what actions the board should consider. In the case of Exercising Authority, should the board undertake a strategic planning process to clarify goals? Should the board initiate a more structured superintendent evaluation?

The board's designee—a consultant, district employee, assessment committee, or other entity—should perform the analysis. This same individual or group then develops a set of possible conclusions and discussion items, organized around each activity area, to frame board discussion of the results.

Action Two: Monitor Progress

The monitoring stage of board improvement is an ongoing review of the board's functioning and progress. The board asks how it is doing and considers whether the answer necessitates a change in current operations. To work, the monitoring process requires asking the question frequently but spending time in comprehensive review only when action is needed. Unlike the self-assessment stage of board improvement, where time is set aside for review, the monitoring should intrude minimally on the day-to-day work of governance.

How can that happen? Each board must decide, but the recommendation here is for a process—a set of questions and a periodic commitment of a few minutes for a review. Here's an example of how it might work.

The process.

The board agrees to a set of questions (no more than five or six) that address the ongoing concerns, as well as those that came out of the self-assessment. Board members receive these questions, in the form of a questionnaire, with their packet of materials every three months. The board president (or designated member of the board) compiles the responses in a brief report and signals any topics for discussion.

The questions.

The questions are of several types:

How are things going?

Are there any issues that are keeping us from functioning effectively as a board?

How are we doing in each of the six areas of effective board activity: making decisions, functioning as a group, exercising authority, connecting to the community, working toward board improvement, and acting strategically?

How are we working against our improvement agenda?

Although generic, the questions can easily be tailored to the specific concerns of each board. For example, one board decides it wants to focus more time on curricular issues, actively reviewing the quality of the instructional program. The questions can specifically address this board priority.

The commitment.

The board agenda includes an item for board performance review. The board discusses the feedback and agrees on any adjustments in board process. If the items are sensitive, involving the actions of individual board members, an agenda item and report can be reserved for a closed board session.

In the example, referring to Exhibits 9.1 and 9.2 where exercising authority was identified as an issue, the questions may ask about the quality of the board-superintendent relationship, about attention to communicating expectations to the superintendent, and about the effectiveness of the superintendent's reflection of board values in recommendations presented for board approval.

Action Three: Develop Systematically

This recommended initiative is a formal, step-by-step process by which boards plan and participate in their own development. There are many approaches to board development. The seven-step process described here includes the essential elements: conduct self-assessment, obtain board commitment to the process, frame the issues, plan a board retreat or conference, conduct the retreat or conference, commit to action, monitor and continue the development cycle.

Conduct self-assessment.

Self-assessment (Action One) has already been described. The purpose of the process is to answer the questions related to where you are now as a board and the issues you face. These issues may relate to the strategic agenda for the school district, to the six areas of effective board action, or to issues such as new board and superintendent roles and governance information.

In the context of a board development program, consider designating the board president and the superintendent to provide initial planning or designate several board members as an ad hoc planning group. They can collect the assessment information and informally probe the more sensitive issues of leadership and collegiality among the board.

Obtain board commitment.

The success of a board development effort depends on the willingness of all members of the board to participate. When board members view the development process as important to effective board operation, they greatly enhance its chances for success. There are always board members who are reluctant participants, particularly at first. But the effort toward board development should not go forward without this commitment.

Frame the issues.

Once the board completes the self-assessment and commits to moving forward, the planning group (superintendent and board president) should coordinate whatever steps are needed to further investigate the issues identified as important for review. Sometimes this may include interviews or focus groups with staff or community, surveys, research on best practices in other districts, or the identification of experts to use as resources. Often a third-party consultant or facilitator is involved in the development process. The role of such a consultant may include independent fact-finding.

This information is then distilled and presented as background and support to assist in board discussion of these issues. Cases may be prepared to describe hypothetical or real situations. Members can use these as a basis for discussion of what they would do under similar circumstances. Those with experience outside the district may organize presentations for possible use in board discussion.

Plan a board retreat or conference.

The centerpiece of a board development program is a retreat or board conference. This is not a regular meeting and should take place at a different, and preferably informal, location. Many boards find an overnight retreat desirable, although not always possible with limited school board budgets. The retreat is often limited to the board members and superintendent, with an outside facilitator (or chair of the ad hoc board planning group) chairing the meeting. The board may invite other resource people to participate in specific portions of the program.

Retreat planning is an important step in the development process. The ad hoc committee specifies the purposes of the retreat and the outcomes expected. Usually the purpose is twofold: one part focused on moving the board's agenda ahead; the other on helping the board function more effectively as a group. So, for example, one purpose might be to establish a strategic five-year direction for the district and another to give board members an opportunity to consider individual priorities and how these fit into this five-year plan.

The planning committee organizes the time available into meeting sessions, thinks through the purposes and outcomes of each session and how each contributes to the whole.

If retained, a consultant often provides leadership to the planning effort. The superintendent is usually a member of the planning group and also often provides leadership.

Conduct the board retreat or conference.

This all leads to the retreat or conference itself—a different experience for each board and in each situation. However, the general format remains similar across different purposes and issues.

Exhibit 9.3 shows an example of a board retreat agenda for the Smithside School District. It was the agenda for an actual retreat, though the format has been slightly modified. The school district has recently hired a new superintendent from outside the district. They plan a Friday and a Saturday morning to think through how they can work together and work with the new superintendent. The board, the superintendent, and a facilitator are the only participants. They use the model proposed in this book as the basis for their discussion. The first day focuses on the board's effectiveness and responsibilities. The second day moves to the issues facing the district and the role of the board in addressing them.

Organize and commit to action.

When the retreat concludes, the planning group assembles the written summaries of group discussions, the actions suggested, and those agreed upon. Participants receive this summary and have a chance to make comments and corrections. Appropriate items are placed on the agenda of the next board meeting for formal action. The committee prepares a plan of action, which takes each recommendation and designates the person responsible for action, the timetable, and the results expected. This becomes the set of indicators against which the board can monitor progress in implementation. Of course, many of the recommendations will be ongoing and involve subtle changes in relationships. (Action Two can assess progress in these areas.)

The board president and superintendent (or the planning group) should also assess the retreat itself. How successful was it? Did it accomplish what participants and planners hoped would be accomplished?

This assessment, shared informally with the board, can form the basis for continued planning for other retreats and conferences that may further board development.

Monitor and continue the development cycle.

Action Two describes the monitoring activity. The results of monitoring progress and board discussion become information that is part of the next

EXHIBIT 9.3

SAMPLE RETREAT AGENDA: Smithside School District School Board Retreat

PURPOSES OF THE RETREAT

- To strengthen the board's working relationship with the new superintendent through a review of its roles and responsibilities.

- To establish specific guidelines to govern the board-superintendent relationship.

- To identify issues the board should address and establish specific priorities and a practical action plan for addressing these issues.

- To enhance collegiality and working relationships among board members.

SCHEDULE

Friday, January 10

10:30 A.M.	Welcome: Board president and superintendent
	Review of retreat purposes and schedule: Retreat facilitator
10:45	What Makes a School Board Effective?
	The facilitator will define and describe the six key dimensions of effective activity associated with high-performing boards. Specific suggestions to improve board performance in each area will be presented, as well as an opportunity for board discussion of the applicability of this information to the Smithside board.
Noon	Lunch
1:00 P.M.	Clarifying Board Responsibilities (I)
	The facilitator will build on the morning discussion by presenting the results of the Smithside Board's self-assessment survey, profiling the results with those of effective boards on the same six key dimensions of effective action. Board members will be asked to identify areas where roles and responsibilities may need clarification and where guidelines may need to be established. A list of "typical" responsibilities will be presented to test the comprehensiveness of the Smithside list. Throughout the discussion, an emphasis will be on the relationship between the board and the superintendent, and the board and the district.
2:00	Clarifying Board Responsibilities (II)
	The board will be divided into two discussion groups of 3-4 persons. These groups were composed in advance by the Retreat Planning Committee. Each group will have a convener to moderate the discussion and a recorder to

report the group's main conclusions orally and in writing. Each group will address the same topics. A list of topics will be prepared by the facilitator.

For each group, start with the areas of responsibility requiring clarification or guidelines as developed in the previous session. For each area, what is the specific rule that should govern board actions, and why? If it is not clear what rule should be established, then what specific steps must be taken to achieve the required clarification; who would be responsible for taking those steps, and in what time frame? Address the areas of highest priority first. Combine areas requiring the same response. Rank order the five most important actions to be taken by the board.

3:30	Break

3:45	Clarifying Board Responsibilities (III)

The reporter for each small group will take up to ten minutes to summarize "our best thinking" on the assigned task and to list "the most promising steps" the board can take to deal with the matter at hand.

Based on these inputs, we will construct a specific, concrete, action-oriented game plan for clarifying board responsibilities and, where necessary, adjusting board operations to support the agreement on responsibilities. We will decide together who needs to do what by when and how the entire follow-up process will be monitored in a way that enables the board to hold itself accountable for instituting these operating rules.

5:15	Refreshments

Saturday, January 11

8:00 A.M.	A Brief Destination Check

Where have we been so far and where are we headed?

8:10 ·	Issues Facing the School District

In advance of the retreat, board members will be asked to comment on the key issues facing the Smithside School District today. This input will be presented in summary form to frame a discussion of issues. The board will be asked to assist in developing a comprehensive list of the most important issues. What are they? Why are they important? Which are the most important and why?

9:30	Small Group Discussion: Board's Role

Using the same groups as Friday, each group will review the listing of important issues, asking these questions: Whose issue is it (that is, what role should

(Continued)

EXHIBIT 9.3 (continued)

the Board play in addressing the issue)? What should the Board do to fulfill its role? What specific actions are required and with what assignment of responsibility and time frame? What is its priority?

Each group should also look at the general question of guidelines that may delineate those issues of proper board concern.

10:45	Break
11:00	Developing an Action Plan
	The reporter for each group will take up to ten minutes to summarize the results of the discussion. Based on this discussion, we will consider guidelines to define issues that are properly within board purview and construct an action plan to address the issues of highest priority. We will decide together what the plan should be to address these issues, with responsibilities, timing, and monitoring specified.
Noon	Summary, Wrap-Up, and Evaluation
	Going around the table, each board member will be asked to comment briefly on the retreat. What was most beneficial? What concerns or apprehensions do you have as we leave?
	Concluding Comments: Board president and superintendent
12:30 P.M.	Adjourn

---

cycle of self-assessment (Step One in the systematic development program). Annually, or over some other prescribed period, the seven-step cycle begins again.

Conclusion

A good development process recognizes the long-term value to the school district of members taking time away from the pressures of public decision making. School boards, like any well-functioning group, need time to reflect—time to determine how to use their partnership with the superintendent and their governance information to improve their effectiveness. The final chapter discusses the next steps for the board.

Conclusion

An Agenda for Action

BOARDS KNOW what effectiveness is, and they have the capacity—potentially—to do the job. That is the overriding conclusion I have drawn from my work. The Model for School Board Effectiveness developed here provides a framework for boards as they work toward more effective action. To perform effectively, boards must have the determination and independence to act based on what they know to be model behavior: they must build partnerships with their superintendents, actively use information as a support, and above all, work diligently for their own development as boards. And boards can do that. Members know what they do when they are effective; many have articulated that knowledge for inclusion in this book.

Boards Can Work

I think the overall picture of school boards and their operation is brighter than many critics contend or than the dramatic publicity of urban dissatisfaction would depict. School boards are perfectly capable of working well. That may simply be the view of an optimist, but I don't think so. I believe the evidence supports it. By their descriptions of particular situations, board members illustrate that they not only know how to behave effectively but sometimes actually do so. The issue is not whether they *can* do the job but whether they *will*. It requires independence and determination, and those qualities are a lot to ask of individuals who emerge in their roles out of a political process and who are volunteers.

A Model for Board Action

The six chapters in Part One describe the Model for School Board Effectiveness. The actions required of boards by this model are summarized in Exhibit C.1.

Importance of board-superintendent partnership.

If the model is to be successfully implemented, boards must first focus on what's important. No model can help a board move forward if it doesn't know where it is going. First, boards should decide what is truly important; next, they should figure out what the board can do that helps or adds

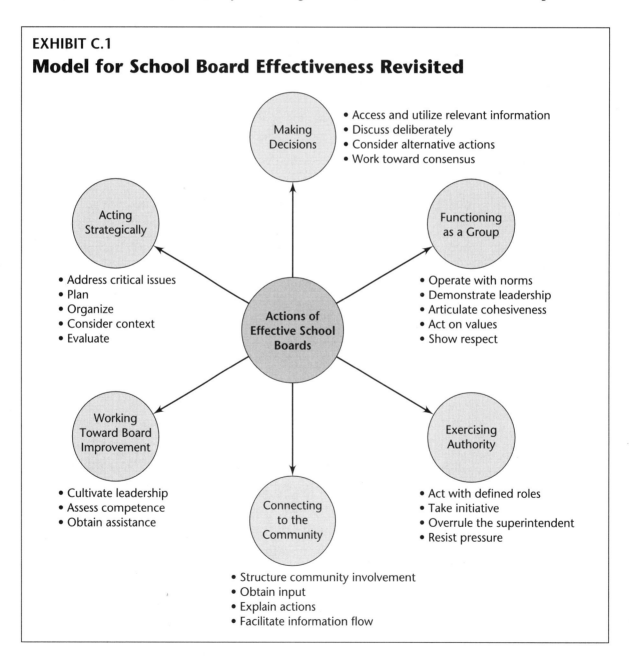

EXHIBIT C.1
Model for School Board Effectiveness Revisited

Making Decisions
- Access and utilize relevant information
- Discuss deliberately
- Consider alternative actions
- Work toward consensus

Acting Strategically
- Address critical issues
- Plan
- Organize
- Consider context
- Evaluate

Actions of Effective School Boards

Functioning as a Group
- Operate with norms
- Demonstrate leadership
- Articulate cohesiveness
- Act on values
- Show respect

Working Toward Board Improvement
- Cultivate leadership
- Assess competence
- Obtain assistance

Connecting to the Community
- Structure community involvement
- Obtain input
- Explain actions
- Facilitate information flow

Exercising Authority
- Act with defined roles
- Take initiative
- Overrule the superintendent
- Resist pressure

value. That will happen when board and superintendent can sort out district business so the board can concentrate on items that shape and support the educational program and performance.

Importance of information.

The quality and appropriateness of information exerts a key influence on school board effectiveness and should focus on what's important. The volume and level of detail should promote critical understanding within reasonable limits of available time. The board should help decide what information is best. The best information helps boards improve their effectiveness.

The board interviews and our discussion illustrate the gap between the requirements of a board member and the qualifications and experience of a new board member. Board members must have the broad perspective of educating all the children in the district. They must be prepared to devote time and energy to understanding and then sensibly resolving key district issues. They must be committed to building a board that can function effectively and with some degree of consensus.

How Boards Can Support Development

So what can boards do to support development? They can—and must—*identify champions* and *form alliances.* Board development becomes an issue of leadership and support. Board members must help their colleagues, their superintendents, and their constituents to understand and support the importance of board improvement and the value of board development activities.

Identify champions.

From the interviews it is clear that when board development took place and was successful, it was because an individual had an idea and persuaded others of its value. To implement board development requires someone who has credibility with the board, has experience with board development activities, and can apply it to a particular situation when the board needs help. Often it is a board member or the superintendent. It can also be a respected member of the community.

Here's one board member's account, which was used earlier (Chapter Six) as an example of a board acting strategically:

> We had a serious problem. The school board members had
> to choose among options for solving the problem. Differences

were deep-rooted. Everyone was frustrated. I threw out on the table the idea of facilitation. I had met with a friend of mine who had a colleague, an expert in human resources. He met with us. The board reached consensus.

Form alliances.

Often, through the network of other nonprofit boards, it is the community that has the experience with board development and the perspective to see its need and value. When strong, respected community leaders advocate board development, board participation becomes a positive step in response to community ideas for improvement. Furthermore, when funds are required for board development, community foundations, business groups, and other organizations can contribute, thus avoiding the controversial use of taxpayer funds for this purpose. Often the community can provide the expertise to conduct development programs.

Several communities have initiated projects to build understanding of what school board governance is and to support school board development:[1]

Grand Rapids, Michigan. The Grand Rapids Public Education Fund (GRPEF) has implemented a school governance initiative. The GRPEF worked with the board of education in helping members see the need to develop a common vision or mission as a governing board. They then contracted with a facilitator to work with the board.

The facilitator worked with the board to develop a governance framework—a common understanding of what the board should do and how it should be organized. She then helped the board develop a governance action plan and indicators of success to measure progress in accomplishing the plan.

Dayton, Ohio. With initiative and funding from the chamber of commerce, the board established a committee of business, school board, and community leaders. This committee retained an outside consulting firm to conduct a study of the district and its board leading to a blueprint for improvement. This blueprint led to passage of a referendum for increased school district funding and an improved understanding of board focus and process.

Seattle, Washington. A task force of local and state leaders, including representatives from major business and community groups, commissioned a comprehensive study that led to recommendations for improved board functioning.

Conclusion

To be effective as a board, individual members should hold a common view of effective board action and discuss how well they are performing and how they can improve. The Model for School Board Effectiveness presented in this book provides a starting place. Its strength is that it emerges from actual board practice and represents a consistency among board members and a perspective confirmed by experts. It now should be tested in actual practice and linked with improved district results—a next step in its evolution.

Appendix A

Methodology

The findings contained in Chapters One through Six are based on extensive interviews with school board members in Delaware. I invited all school board members in the state to interview. Forty-five of the 117 were interviewed, and these included at least one board member from all but one of the districts in the state.

I interviewed each school board member in person; interviews generally lasted between one and two hours. I used a structured but open-ended interview protocol. A copy of this protocol is included as Exhibit A.1.[1] The interviews centered on an adaptation of the *critical incident* technique, which asked school board members to describe and discuss in detail situations in which they were effective as school board members and as a school board. In most interviews two researchers were present. Each recorded in writing the conversation as it occurred, and the two versions were compared to ensure accuracy.

These interview notes were reviewed in detail. Common themes were identified. The reported actions of school board members were identified and combined into areas that captured activities that were integral to effective boards. Then the analysis proceeded in two parts. First, the answers to the general questions in the interview protocol were analyzed as context to the more specific situational responses. Second, code words were assigned to the areas of activity of effective boards that had been identified, and these code words were defined and then used to represent the specific areas of effective action. Using a software program, "Ethnograph," produced by Qualis Research Associates in Amherst, Massachusetts, the interview text that described critical incidents was coded so that the portions of the description illustrating particular activities were identified. The software enabled me to sort this material by activity. That way I could count the number of times these activities occurred and organize descriptions by coded category. Text was coded in a fashion that enabled certain descriptions to be multiple-coded. Overall, 111 incidents were identified in the interview notes, and each of these was multiple-coded by activity. In a qualitative, iterative process, the code words and their definitions were refined, based on closer analysis of the text, and became the framework for the Model for School Board Effectiveness. The results of this analysis are described in Chapters One through Six.

A word of justification for this methodology is in order. It is grounded in the qualitative method that suggests beginning with specific cases (here, incidences of school board effectiveness) and identifying universal themes—activities that carry across these cases as the basis of a model for further testing. This methodology is theoretically justified and is also a rich narrative for school board members to review as they seek an understanding of what they do and how they can do it better.

The use of the critical incident methodology has been well documented in the literature.[2] I drew directly from its use by the researchers who had developed a model for the effectiveness of trustees.[3]

The analysis in this book makes two assumptions, which should be tested through further research and warrant brief discussion here. The first is that effective school board action is what I have described it to be. Our evidence is based on what school board members say and our own sense of what works, based on discussion with experts, many years of consulting with school districts, and the written accounts of researchers and journalists about school board activity. There is a need to confirm our claim of face validity.

The second assumption is that the school board experience reflected by extensive interviews in Delaware reflects experience throughout the country. The mix of urban, suburban, and rural districts suggests that this is so. Again, the prima facie review of descriptions corresponds with testimony of experts and the author's national consulting experience. However, this assumption also needs confirmation. In particular, researchers should test whether the Delaware experience can encompass the largest urban districts nationally, with school board members who are paid, connected with city politics, and able to devote full-time to their work.

Of course, face validity should be but a first step in determining school board effectiveness. The more fundamental question is: What are the characteristics of school boards' behavior that can be linked with student achievement or other indicators of district success? Demonstrating that effective board behavior corresponds with districts that have students with a high rate of achievement, corrected for differences in background or ability, would be stronger proof that the effectiveness model is valid.

EXHIBIT A.1

Interview Protocol

This exhibit presents the interview protocol used for each of the forty-five interviewees from Delaware school boards. For each interviewee there are two sections: the first consists of general comments organized as answers to specific questions. They are coded according to categories.

How Boards Function: A View from the Field

Why Do Board Members Serve?

Why do people vote for them?

What Do They Find Satisfying About Their Jobs?

What do they find frustrating?

How Do They Learn Their Jobs?

How can they improve?

What Working Relationships Do They Establish?

In their own work together

In their relationship with the board president

In their work with the superintendent

In their work with the community

In their work with the legislature

How Do They Make Decisions?

How do they deal with crises?

How do they use information?

How Do They Define Their Scope of Responsibilities?

How do they define their effectiveness?

How Do They Describe Their Rules of Operation?

How Do They Describe Their Climate/Culture?

How Do They Describe Their Roles In

Strategic planning

Shaping program

Connecting with community

Accountability

How Do They Define

Leadership

Underlying values

The role of the superintendent

The role of the board president

What Resources Do They Use?

How Do They Evaluate Their Effectiveness?

The second section describes specific critical incidents (called cases). To collect this information, I used an interview protocol. A copy of this protocol is as follows:

___

Delaware School Boards Project
Interview Guide

1.   Introduction

1.1   I am. . . .

1.2   We are trying to learn in some detail what makes a school board effective. At the conclusion of the project we hope that we will be able to describe an effective board and identify those factors that contribute most significantly to a board's effectiveness. This information will, we hope, help boards improve their performance and in that way strengthen education in their school districts.

1.3   At this early stage of our work, we are collecting information that will help us develop a framework of effectiveness that we can test later on. We are interviewing several school board members for a number of school districts. We think that people such as yourself are in an unusually good position to comment on what makes a school board more or less effective.

1.4   This interview will take about an hour. I will be taking notes for later use in writing about our findings. Everything you say will be considered confidential. Your school district will be identified as a participant in the project, but all material used in our

(Continued)

EXHIBIT A.1 (continued)

study will be presented in a manner that will not permit the identification of any school district or person.

1.5 Before we begin, do you have any questions about the project?

2.   Background

2.1 When were you appointed/elected to the board? How many terms/years have you served?

2.2 Why were you appointed/elected? Why were you chosen for an additional term?

2.3 What was your experience with the school district before joining the board?

3.   Exchange

3.1 Why did you agree to serve?

3.2 What have you found to be the most satisfying or fulfilling aspects of your work on the board?

3.3 When your term on the board expires, would you seek or agree to another term? If so, why?

3.4 What have you found to be the most frustrating or disappointing aspects of service on the board?

4.   Critical Incidents

4.1 Sometimes it is easier to get a clear picture of how a school board works and what a school board does by discussing something very concrete. Would you take a few minutes now to recall three key situations in the past 2–3 years where you think the board was particularly effective in dealing with an important matter. You may wish to jot down key words as reminders for each incident. (Pause several minutes.)

4.2 Of the three incidents let's start with the most recent.

4.2.1 When did this event occur?

4.2.2 What were the general circumstances leading up to this event?

4.3 Please describe the event in detail.

4.3.1 What did this specific incident concern?

4.3.2	Who was involved?
4.3.3	Was the board as a whole involved or only certain board members?
4.4	Please describe the board's involvement in detail.
4.4.1	When did the board (or board members) become involved?
4.4.2	How did the board (or board members) become involved?
4.4.3	Why did the board (or board members) become involved?
4.5	What specifically did the board (or board members) do in handling this event?
4.5.1	What actions did the board (or members) take?
4.5.2	What did the board (or members) say to whom?
4.5.3	What rationale was used in determining who would do or say what?
4.6	What do you think the board wanted to accomplish in this situation?
4.7	What makes you think that the board's handling of this event was "effective"?
4.8	What in your opinion best explains why the board was able to handle this event effectively?
4.9	Now I would like to ask the same questions about the second/third critical incident.

5. *Leadership*

5.1	How would you describe the operating style and pattern of the board?
5.2	How important is the board to what goes on in the district?
5.3	How would you describe the operating relationship between the board and the superintendent?
5.4	How important is that relationship to what goes on in the district?
5.5	How does the board know if it is providing effective leadership?
5.6	What would you consider the single biggest mistake the board has made—if you had it to do all over again, what would you do differently?
5.7	What steps should be taken to improve the effectiveness of the board?

(Continued)

EXHIBIT A.1 (continued)

6.   *District Differentiation*

6.1   How is your school district different from other school districts in the state and nationally?

6.2   How would you distinguish your board, its style of operation, and the issues it faces from boards of other districts in the state and nationally?

7.   *Conclusion*

7.1   Is there anything else you would like to say about the effectiveness of school boards in general?

7.2   Thank you very much for your time and thoughts.

Source: Protocol based on personal communication with and unpublished research material developed by Richard P. Chait, Thomas P. Holland, and Barbara E. Taylor, in a study conducted at the National Center for Postsecondary Governance and Finance, University of Maryland. Used by permission of the researchers.

The Board Self-Assessment Questionnaire

Thank you for participating in this self-assessment of your school board. The following statements describe a variety of possible actions by boards. Some of the statements may represent your own experiences as a member of your board, while others may not. For each of the items, there are four possible choices. Please mark with a check (✓) the choice which most accurately describes your experience as a member of this board.

There are no "right" or "wrong" answers; your personal views are what is important. In order to ensure the anonymity of all responses, please do not put your name anywhere on the form. After you have completed all the items, please fold the form, insert it into the envelope provided, and drop it in the mail. Thank you.

	Strongly Agree	Agree	Disagree	Strongly Disagree
1. This board works to reach consensus on important matters.				
2. I have participated in board discussions about what we should do differently as a result of a mistake the board made.				
3. There have been occasions where the board itself has acted in ways inconsistent with the district's deepest values.				
4. This board has formal structures and procedures for involving the community.				

Note: Adapted from material originally developed by the Center for Higher Education Governance and Leadership, University of Maryland, College Park, under funding by the Lilly Endowment. Used by permission of Tom Holland.

	Strongly Agree	Agree	Disagree	Strongly Disagree
5. I have been in board meetings where it seemed that the subtleties of the issues we dealt with escaped the awareness of a number of the members.				
6. Our board explicitly examines the "downside" or possible pitfalls of any important decision it is about to make.				
7. Usually the board and superintendent advocate the same actions.				
8. This board is more involved in trying to put out fires than in preparing for the future.				
9. The board sets clear organizational priorities for the year ahead.				
10. A written report including the board's activities is periodically prepared and distributed publicly.				
11. This board communicates its decisions to all those who are affected by them.				
12. At least once every two years, our board has a retreat or special session to examine our performance, how well we are doing as a board.				
13. Many of the issues that this board deals with seem to be separate tasks, unrelated to one another.				
14. The board will sharply question certain administrative proposals, requiring the superintendent to reconsider the recommendations.				
15. The board is always involved in decisions that are important to the future of education in our district.				
16. If our board thinks that an important group of constituents is likely to disagree with an action we are considering, we will make sure we learn how they feel before we actually make the decision.				
17. Board members don't say one thing in private and another thing in public.				
18. This board and its members maintain channels of communication with specific key community leaders.				

	Strongly Agree	Agree	Disagree	Strongly Disagree
19. This board delays action until an issue becomes urgent or critical.				
20. This board periodically sets aside time to learn more about important issues facing school districts like the one we govern.				
21. This board relies on the natural emergence of leaders rather than trying explicitly to cultivate future leaders for the board.				
22. This board has formed ad hoc committees or task forces that include staff and community representatives as well as board members.				
23. This board is as attentive to how it reaches conclusions as it is to what is decided.				
24. The decisions of this board on one issue tend to influence what we do about other issues that come before us.				
25. Most people on this board tend to rely on observation and informal discussions to learn about their roles and responsibilities.				
26. This board's decisions usually result in a split vote.				
27. When faced with an important issue, the board often "brainstorms" and tries to generate a whole list of creative approaches or solutions to the problem.				
28. When a new member joins this board, we make sure that someone serves as a mentor to help this person learn the ropes.				
29. I have been in board meetings where explicit attention was given to the concerns of the community.				
30. I rarely disagree openly with other members in board meetings.				
31. I have participated in board discussions about the effectiveness of our performance.				

	Strongly Agree	Agree	Disagree	Strongly Disagree
32. At our board meetings, there is at least as much dialogue among members as there is between members and administrators.				
33. A certain group of board members will usually vote together for or against particular issues.				
34. I have participated in discussions with new members about the roles and responsibilities of a board member.				
35. The board will often persuade the superintendent to change his mind about recommendations.				
36. The leadership of this board typically goes out of its way to make sure that all members have the same information on important issues.				
37. The board has adopted some explicit goals for itself, distinct from goals it has for the total school district.				
38. The board often requests that a decision be postponed until further information can be obtained.				
39. The board periodically obtains information on the perspectives of staff and community.				
40. This board seeks outside assistance in considering its work.				
41. Our board meetings tend to focus more on current concerns than on preparing for the future.				
42. At least once a year, this board asks that the superintendent articulate his/her vision for the school district's future and strategies to realize that vision.				
43. The board often requests additional information before making a decision.				
44. I have never received feedback on my performance as a member of this board.				
45. The board often discusses its role in district management.				
46. This board has on occasion evaded responsibility for some important issue facing the school district.				

	Strongly Agree	Agree	Disagree	Strongly Disagree
47. Before reaching a decision on important issues, this board usually requests input from persons likely to be affected by the decision.				
48. Recommendations from the administration are usually accepted with little questioning.				
49. Board members are consistently able to hold confidential items in confidence.				
50. This board often discusses where the school district should be headed five or more years into the future.				
51. The board president and superintendent confer so that differences of opinion are identified.				
52. This board does not allocate organizational funds for the purpose of board education and development.				
53. I have been present in board meetings where discussions of the values of the district were key factors in reaching a conclusion on a problem.				
54. The board usually receives a full rationale for the recommendations it is asked to act upon.				
55. At times this board has appeared unaware of the impact its decisions will have within our service community.				
56. Within the past year, this board has reviewed the school district's strategies for attaining its long-term goals.				
57. We are not a "rubber stamp" board.				
58. This board has conducted an explicit examination of its roles and responsibilities.				
59. I am able to speak my mind on key issues without fear that I will be ostracized by some members of this board.				
60. This board tries to avoid issues that are ambiguous and complicated.				
61. The administration rarely reports to the board on the concerns of those the school district serves.				

	Strongly Agree	Agree	Disagree	Strongly Disagree
62. I have been in board meetings where the discussion focused on identifying or overcoming the school district's weaknesses.				
63. This board often acts independent of the superintendent's recommendations.				
64. Values are seldom discussed explicitly at our board meetings.				
65. This board spends a lot of time listening to different points of view before it votes on an important matter.				
66. The board discusses events and trends in the larger environment that may present specific opportunities for this school district.				
67. The board is outspoken in its views about programs.				
68. Once a decision is made, all board members work together to see that it is accepted and carried out.				
69. All board members support majority decisions.				
70. This board makes explicit use of the long-range priorities of this school district in dealing with current issues.				
71. The board will reverse its position based on pressure from the community.				
72. Members of this board are sometimes disrespectful in their comments to other board members.				
73. More than half of this board's time is spent in discussions of issues of importance to the school district's long-range future.				

Scoring the Questionnaire

The seventy-three questions in the self-assessment questionnaire each address an activity related to one of the six elements of the Model for School Board Effectiveness. The questions can be grouped according to the following elements:

Making Decisions: 1, <u>5</u>, 6, <u>13</u>, 24, <u>26</u>, 27, <u>33</u>, 38, 54, <u>60</u>, 65, 69

Functioning as a Group: 3, 17, <u>30</u>, 32, 36, 37, 49, 53, 59, <u>64</u>, 68, <u>72</u>

Exercising Authority: 7, 14, 15, <u>35</u>, 43, 45, <u>48</u>, 51, 57, 63, 67, <u>71</u>

Connecting to the Community: 4, 10, 11, 16, 18, 22, 23, 29, 39, 47, <u>55</u>, <u>61</u>

Working Toward Board Improvement: 2, 12, 20, <u>21</u>, <u>25</u>, 28, 31, 34, 40, <u>44</u>, <u>52</u>, 58

Acting Strategically: <u>8</u>, 9, <u>19</u>, <u>41</u>, 42, <u>46</u>, 50, 56, 62, 66, 70, 73

   The questions are scored as follows: If a school board member responds "Strongly Disagree" on an item, the item is scored as zero (0). A response of "Disagree" is scored as 1. "Agree" equals a score of 2, and "Strongly Agree" equals 3. The cumulative score for all respondents is then averaged and divided by 3 to obtain a percentage of the highest possible score by the group. Questions that are underlined are "reverse scored." This means that the proper response is in the negative, so "Strongly Agree" is scored a zero (0), "Agree" a 1, "Disagree" a 2, and "Strongly Disagree" a 3.

   For comparison purposes, use an average response of "2" or "Agree." Then you can examine, for your board's total response and for the board's response on each of the six areas, how well the board scored by comparison with a response in keeping with the effectiveness model.

   Exhibits 9.1 and 9.2 illustrate the graphic display of this information.

Source: Format adapted from "Assessment of Board Performance," Holland, Blackmon & Assocs., Inc., Athens, Georgia, February, 1998, unpublished report. Used by permission of Holland, Blackmon & Associates, Inc.

Notes

Preface

1. "Education Vital Signs." *American School Board Journal,* Dec. 1996, *183*(12), A20. See also "Table 5: Distribution of Regular Public Elementary and Secondary School Districts and Students by District Membership Size: School Year 1995–96." U.S. Department of Education, National Center for Education Statistics, Common Core of Data, Agency Universe, 1995–96.

2. See recommendations contained in Danzberger, J. P., Kirst, M. W., and Usdan, M. D. *Governing Public Schools.* Washington, D.C.: Institute for Educational Leadership, 1992. See also background discussion in Wirt, F. M., and Kirst, M. W., *The Political Dynamics of American Education.* Berkeley, Calif.: McCutchan, 1997.

3. See, for example, Harrington-Lueker, D. "School Boards at Bay." *American School Board Journal,* May 1996, *183*(5), 18–22.

4. Smoley, E. R. *New Directions, Board Operations, and Development Priorities.* Research and Development Center, University of Delaware, 1994.

5. The self-assessment questionnaire and the criteria used in the self-assessment are based on material developed in a study of boards of trustees conducted at the National Center for Postsecondary Governance and Finance, University of Maryland. The concepts and methodology are based on personal communication with the principal researchers for this study and on unpublished research materials they developed. The results of their work are contained in Chait, R. P., Holland, T. P., and Taylor, B. E., *The Effective Board of Trustees.* New York: American Council on Education and Macmillan, 1991. The concepts are further developed, along with a version of the self-assessment questionnaire, in Chait,

Holland, and Taylor, *Improving the Performance of Governing Boards.* Phoenix: American Council on Education and Oryx Press, 1996.

Introduction: Why School Boards Fail

1. Danzberger, J. P., Kirst, M. W., and Usdan, M. D. *Governing Public Schools.* See also First, P. F., and Walberg, H. J. (eds.), *School Boards: Changing Local Control*, Berkeley, Calif.: McCutchan, 1992.

2. Bruni, F. "City Offers Preview of Bilingual Education Battle," *New York Times*, May 27, 1998, p. A12.

3. See the discussion of the fifteen indicators in "Indicators of School Board Effectiveness," Danzberger, J. P., Kirst, M. W., and Usdan, M. D., pp. 55–56 and 66–80. See also *Becoming A Better Board Member*, Alexandria, Va.: National School Boards Association, 1996, 8–10. Other sources include Houle, C. O., *Governing Boards: Their Nature and Nurture.* San Francisco: Jossey-Bass, 1989; Ingram, R. T., *Ten Basic Responsibilities of Nonprofit Boards.* Washington, D.C.: National Center for Nonprofit Boards, 1990; The Cheswick Center, "Trusteeship in Troubled Waters," unpublished conference notes, Mar. 1996; Smoley, E. R., *School Board Development: Needs and Opportunities.* Washington, D.C.: National Center for Nonprofit Boards, 1996.

Chapter Five: Working Toward Board Improvement

1. "Education Vital Signs." *American School Board Journal*, Dec. 1996, *183*(12), A20. Interviewees cited and confirmed both the time required to understand roles and the method for learning their responsibilities.

2. Robinson, G. E., and Bickers, P. M., *Evaluation of Superintendents and School Boards.* Arlington, Va.: Educational Research Service, 1990; Carol, L. N., and others, *School Boards: Strengthening Grass Roots Leadership.* Washington, D.C.: The Institute for Educational Leadership, 1992; Smoley, E. R., *School Board Development: Needs and Opportunities.* Washington, D.C.: National Center for Nonprofit Boards, 1996.

Chapter Seven: Strengthening the Superintendent-Board Partnership

1. See Taylor, B. E., Chait R. P., and Holland, T. P. "The New Work of the Nonprofit Board," *Harvard Business Review*, Sept.-Oct. 1996 (reprint 96509). A somewhat similar concept is reflected in Goodman, R. H., Fulbright, L., and Zimmerman, W. G., Jr. *Getting There From Here.* Arlington, Va.: New England School Development Council and

Educational Research Service, 1997. See also Lorsch, J. W., "Empowering the Board," *Harvard Business Review.* Jan.-Feb. 1995, 107–117, (reprint 95107) for a discussion of the concept as it applies to corporate boards.

2. This concept is articulated in Taylor, Chait, and Holland, "The New Work of the Nonprofit Board."

Chapter Eight: Getting the Best Information

1. The critical importance of information and agenda are highlighted in Savage, T. J., *Seven Steps to a More Effective Board.* Kansas City: The Cheswick Center/National Press Publications, 1994. For a comprehensive analysis of board information systems, see Butler, L. M., Hirsch, G. B., and Swift, S. S., *Board Information Systems,* Rockville, Md.: The Cheswick Center, 1995 (unpublished). (The Cheswick Center, 11140 Rockville Pike, #316, Rockville, MD 20852; telephone 301/770-6272.) See also *A View From Inside the BIS Project: A Report to Lilly Endowment, Inc.* Rockville, Md.: The Cheswick Center, 1996.

2. Lorsch, J. W. "Empowering the Board," *Harvard Business Review.* Jan.-Feb. 1995, 115 (reprint 95107).

3. I am greatly indebted to Larry Butler for highlighting and documenting the importance of this concept. The quote is from Butler, Hirsch, and Swift, *Board Information Systems*, p. 69.

4. Butler, Hirsch, and Swift, *Board Information Systems*, pp. 4–5.

5. Butler suggests similar criteria in Butler, Hirsch, and Swift, *Board Information Systems*.

Chapter Nine: Engaging in Board Development

1. The evidence cited here is from a recent project I conducted for the National Center for Nonprofit Boards under Lilly Endowment support. The purpose of this project was to examine the needs and opportunities for school board development. We convened a resource panel, and I conducted interviews with more than forty experts, association executives, and school board members. See Smoley, E. R., *School Board Development: Needs and Opportunities.* Washington, D.C.: National Center for Nonprofit Boards, 1996.

2. Tallerico, M. "The Professional Development of School Board Members." *Journal of Staff Development,* Winter 1993, 14(1), 32–36; Smoley, E. R., *School Board Development: Needs and Opportunities.* Washington, D.C.: National Center for Nonprofit Boards, 1996.

3. Holland, Blackmon & Associates, Inc., have developed a computer model and service to score and display the information graphically in a comprehensive report format that frames the questions for discussion prompted by the self-assessment. (Holland, Blackmon & Associates, Inc., P.O. Box 1002, Athens, GA 30603; telephone 706/548-4115)

Conclusion: An Agenda for Action

1. These examples are cited in Smoley, E. R., *School Board Development: Needs and Opportunities*, pp. 17–18.

Appendix A: Methodology

1. For the results of a study using a similar protocol, see Chait, R. P., Holland, T. P., and Taylor, B. E., *The Effective Board of Trustees*. New York: American Council on Education and Macmillan, 1991.

2. Flanagan, J. C. "The Critical Incident Technique," *Psychological Bulletin*, July 1954, *51*(4), 327–358.

3. See Chait, Holland, and Taylor, *The Effective Board of Trustees*.